SHINZEN KARATE

Title: Shinzen Karate
Genre: Non-Fiction
Desc: Learn the basics of effective self-defense. Shinzen Karate is a power style of Karate based on the teachings of Sosai Masutatsu Oyama.
Author: Kambiz Mostofizadeh
Publisher: Mikazuki Publishing House
ISBN-13: 978-0-9910285-8-0
Date Published: 2018

Disclaimer: This book is for entertainment purposes only.

SOCIAL MEDIA
Facebook.com/MikazukiPublishingHouse
Instagram.com/MikazukiPublishingHouse

SHINZEN KARATE

TABLE OF CONTENTS

SHINZEN KARATE

The Shinzen Karate patch as given to me when I received my 1st Dan Black Belt in Shinzen Karate from the International Shinzen Karate Organization in March 2003.

SHINZEN KARATE

INTRODUCTION

I started training in Martial Arts at the tender age of 4, when my Mother signed me up for Tae Kwan Do classes in Woodland Hills, California at Simon Rhee Tae Kwan Do. Simon Rhee is not only a teacher but is also a famous award winning fight choreographer (Lethal Weapon 4, Blade 2, Inception). Simon Rhee is known for having the most technical kicking form and finesse. Simon Rhee was a heavy influence on me as a child and I remember spending hours in the backyard of my parents home practicing Kata. The movements would quiet my mind and make me focus. It also taught me techniques at a young age that I would be using in real fighting later on. I did get in 7 street fights in my youth and the only person that did manage to beat me up was a Korean in the 7th grade. I may have blocked the first three punches he threw with perfect outside blocks but one of his punches managed to hit me in the nose. My

SHINZEN KARATE

nose started bleeding and the fight was
over. We became friends after the fight,
which is usually what happens when
children fight. After the fight he invited me
to his house and offered me fruit and soft
drinks, like we were old pals. In 2018 I
imagine, there would be an international
incident created if two children get in to a
school fight, but when I was a child, it was
all part of growing up. He wasn't really a
bully and I wasn't really a tough guy, we just
both wanted to act cool. But learning Tae
Kwan Do as a child did allow me to defend
myself on several occasions in my teens
against bigger opponents. I was jumped by
a gang in Melrose Avenue in Los Angeles,
California when I was in my late teens and I
was able to defend myself alone against 3
opponents. I punched two of the opponents
and front kicked another, buying me
enough time to get to safety. I was able to
fight all three opponents because I had
trained for many years prior to that incident
and I was not afraid of fighting a bully. Since

SHINZEN KARATE

I was not in the wrong and I was in the right, the opponent was the bully and I was defending myself. Martial Arts gives you that confidence to protect yourself when you most need it. If you think training is difficult, then think about what you will do if you are attacked by 3 or 4 or 5 thugs and you are with your family. Martial Arts training is not for social media bragging, it is for your protection during times of life and death. As a child, I was amazed by movies that showed a Martial Artist able to defend themselves against multiple opponents and walk away unscathed. There is something magical about martial arts when one is a child or a teen. It is almost unable to describe. The grace, the finesse, the perfectly executed movements, and the efficiency of it, make it a truly unique human activity. Simon Rhee is Korean as was Sosai Masutatsu Oyama who was the founder of Kyokushin Karate. The Koreans have a fighting spirit that is to be admired and their martial arts are efficient and

SHINZEN KARATE

technical. Mas Oyama, in his book titled "This Is Karate" stated that you should "Concentrate on sincerity and on unifying your spirit. Forget yourself, forget your enemies, forget winning and losing, and when you have done so, you will be in the spiritually unified state that is called Mu , or nothingness, in Zen. When you have spiritually reached the state of impassivity you will have entered a corner of the Zen world of mu. We can reach this stage of impassivity whether we are eating or working. When one is writing or when one is working if he works with enthusiasm but forgets that he is actually working, he has achieved a state of Zen". Ideas like these can be foreign to the Western mind but a little concentration on their meaning reveals much about their concepts. It is important to understand the Asian mind that created the style of Karate. It was the Asian continent that gave life to Karate and with its creation came the values that defined it. Karate is an Asian phenomenon

SHINZEN KARATE

that spread throughout Asia and took on
different names depending on the nation it
was practiced in. The Asian philosophy of
War values the value of Peace higher above
all values. This value, among other values,
spread throughout Dojos in Asia, Europe,
Australia, North America, and South
America. Wherever a Dojo existed, you
could hear words like "Sensei" and "Osu"
and "Rei" being used. Japanese values and
Japanese culture defined Karate in its
traditional and still define Karate in its
modern Olympic form. Karate schools,
whether they are in Japan or in China or in
the U.S., still count their training in
Japanese. Japanese words are still used to
name techniques during testing. Thousands
of people every year travel to Okinawa,
Japan to train authentic Japanese Karate.
Japan is the recognized birthplace and
home of the martial art and sport of Karate.
People ridicule and make fun of things they
don't understand and Karate is no
exception to the ill humor. The Japanese

SHINZEN KARATE

take Karate very seriously, the way that Americans take American Football seriously. Karate is viewed as a National Sport in Japan and any foreign criticism of Karate is viewed as an attack on the Japanese culture and the Japanese way of life. Karate is a way of life that has been practiced, in one form or another, for thousands of years. It is the art of using the empty hand and foot to defend oneself from the perils that life presents. Through the study of Karate, you can achieve a peaceful state of mind, a balanced character, a healthier body, and the self confidence to defend yourself and your loved ones, should the need arise. Despite the vast amount of techniques that this book could have discussed, it is very important to understand that in Karate, the mastering of less techniques takes precedence over mediocre application of all techniques. If you are able to masterfully execute 15 techniques, you will have 15 techniques in your Karate arsenal for self defense. But to attempt to master everything, will make you mediocre at everything. Each technique and/or movement in Karate should be mastered before attempting to move on to the next. It is fine to pick 3-4 techniques to focus on at any given period of time, master them, then move on to mastering new techniques. Karate, having stemmed from the Shaolin Temple in China, encompassed a vast amount of techniques in their syllabus. Some Karate styles have a longer syllabus and some have a shorter syllabus. Whether the style requires the memorization and execution of many techniques or few techniques, the smaller amount of techniques you truly master will be worth more to you in a confrontation than knowing hundreds of techniques that you have a low level of proficiency in. Training constantly is the most important element to your success as a Karateka. Karate has no shortcuts and no stepping stones. It is a lifelong journey and your rate of advancement in this journey will be

SHINZEN KARATE

dictated by the hours spent mastering its techniques. It is a process that develops the student in to a proficient Karateka over time. It takes real effort, physical and mental to learn Karate. Karate has to be learned in an authentic and real manner for it to be applicable in a situation that requires its use. You can't build a Karateka overnight or in a few short sessions. It takes many thousands of hours to develop proficiency in kicking. According to Sosai Masutatsu Oyama, it takes ten thousands days of training to achieve mastery. Ten thousands days would be approximately thirty years of training, which would mean a student would have to spend their entire lifetime training to claim mastery of Karate. If in the early 20th century you were lucky enough to find a Karate school with an authentic Karate teacher to guide you, you would have to seek permission to be accepted. If you were accepted, you would be taught very little at a time and you would spend many hours carrying out the

SHINZEN KARATE

various tasks the Sensei or Cohai would assign to you. Your learning was done in a gradual and slow manner so that what you learned would soak and be retainable by you. It was slow, tedious, time consuming, and probably exhausting. Many Uchi Deshi or Live In Students spent their entire time in training and working. Their tasks in a day could include everything from picking rice, cooking food, gathering firewood, or tending to other menial chores. This type of training instilled discipline in young apprentices of the Sensei who sought to emulate his success and his way of life. In fact, every lesson taught by the Sensei was an opportunity by the student to change their mode of thinking and their style to that of Sensei. The Sensei was the living breathing manifestation of character, courage, compassion, honor, and respect. The Sensei personified what the student could attain if they maintained a life of discipline and serious work. The Sensei would teach the student how to think and

SHINZEN KARATE

how to walk. The student was required to forgo their past life and take on the new way of the Sensei teaching them. Instruction in manners, instruction in human values that shape the character, and instruction in the many techniques of Karate helped the student transform and mature. Karate helped the student achieve greatness by the Sensei tapping in to the human potential of the student. Karate was practiced, not talked about. In modern times, Karateka will lecture endlessly about Karate. In ancient times, Karate was practiced instead of being lectured about. Karate skills would be honed through endless hours of practice so that each student would be prepared for being tested by the Sensei and other senior students. Karateka became Black Belts by being tested in the Dojo by senior students as well as being certified by the Sensei. The Sensei would sign and hand deliver the certification scroll to the student as a ritual. Techniques were passed on orally instead of

SHINZEN KARATE

being written down. Except for the Bubishi, little or no books were passed on from ancient times that specifically showed Karate. Karate was passed on in oral tradition and Karate dojos in Okinawa were semi-formal and not highly organized. It was through the physical practice of Karate that Karate was passed on in tradition. It was through the practice of Karate in Dojos that Karate grew in popularity. The more Dojos that opened, the more that Karate grew in popularity. Sparring trained students to fight and gave them applicable experience in attacking and defending against a real time opponent. No one in the history of Karate has ever learned Karate from reading a book. You can only learn Karate from an authentic Karate teacher with an advanced degree in Karate. In my opinion, you should travel to Okinawa, Japan and learn Karate. This would be the ideal place to learn it. Do not buy this book hoping to learn Karate. Karate should be learned in a Dojo. This book is for people

SHINZEN KARATE

that want a general understanding of Shinzen Karate, an off-shoot style of Mas Oyama's Kyokushin Karate. The specific difference between Mas Oyama's Kyokushin Karate and Shinzen Karate is in the percentage of foot/hand techniques used. Although Kyokushin Karate stressed the use of feet in attack, Mas Oyama himself preferred to punch and knockout opponents. Karate literally means "Empty Hand" in Japanese. Shinzen Karate carried on this lineage by focusing on hand techniques with a 70 percent focus on hands and 30 percent focus on feet. The style of Shinzen Karate , created by Kancho Youssef Shirzad, was established in 1973 based on the teachings of Sosai Masutatsu Oyama. In fact, Kancho Youssef Shirzad was a live-in student (uchi deshi) of Mas Oyama. This book is for enjoyment and for reflection upon that which you are already learning in your Karate dojo. Not all Karate styles were created equally. Some focus more on foot attacks, some focus more on

SHINZEN KARATE

Kata, and some focus more on hand attacks. Shinzen Karate incorporates the sport element of Karate while maintaining the traditional and authentic roots which created it. As a Karateka, you should train seriously and train regularly. The more that you train, the more that you will develop a deeper understanding of the techniques your are practicing. Karate should not only be practiced physically but it should be practiced mentally. Your mind should be performing the Karate in thought and in vision. Training Karate is about being able to get rid of any and all distractions and being able to focus on the techniques while you are practicing them. Karateka became Black Belts by polishing and honing their techniques in Kata and Jiyu Kumite. If you want to become a Karate Black Belt, then you have to be willing to put in the hard work and to have the dedication to achieve success. You should train with focus and dedication to your art. Karate is an art, a Martial Art, which requires tens of

SHINZEN KARATE

thousands of days of practice before serious proficiency can be acquired in its correct application. Train diligently, train intelligently, and train with sincerity. No Karate Black Belts are created overnight. You cannot jump forward in Belts because you won a tournament or did really well in sparring. Karate has a syllabus just like any academic study and it is by following this syllabus that the knowledge Karate contains can be passed on in an organized manner. Karate Teachers have a Lineage that is followed in order to understand the Teachers that came before them and to better be able to impart the knowledge they received. A Martial Artists' first dedication is to Peace. Peace creates balance and balance creates happiness. Karate is not a brutish activity because the main focus of Karate is the refinement of the human character in the values of courage, compassion, honor, and respect. Karateka do have higher characters than your average person and that is because the

SHINZEN KARATE

hard training of the Dojo has broken their egos and built their bodies through hard training. Their minds and characters are built through the practice of the values that define Karate. The closest thing to a modern Karate Black Belt would be a 16th Century Village Sherriff. In fact many martial artists were used throughout history as local authorities to quell riots or prevent bloodshed. The Shaolin Monks were used frequently as such type authorities. There are some experts that claim that Karate evolved out of White Crane Kung Fu which was a branch of the Shaolin Temple style of fighting. Even if this were true, Karate was created in Japan and was then and is now a uniquely Japanese martial art. Karate, out of necessity, did incorporate techniques from the Shaolin Temple as it is widely known that Chuan Fa (Kung Fu) became Kempo in Japan. Kempo was the Japanese pronunciation for Chuan Fa (Kung Fu). Kempo Karate translated in to "Kung Fu Chinese Hand". It wasn't until Japanese

SHINZEN KARATE

sentiments of nationalism played in that the word Karate was changed from "Chinese Hand" to "Empty Hand". Chinese martial arts preceded Japanese martial arts and it can be said with certainty that the Chinese laid the base for the future development of Karate. But Karate was given uniquely Japanese characteristics during its development in to its current modern form. The Chinese knew full well of the potential of Karate to stop bandits and local criminals. Karateka were not only authorities but they were also bonesetters. It was expected that the Karateka that could break bones could also heal bones. It was created for Peace. Karate Ni Sente Nashi means "There is no first strike in Karate". I want to remind the martial artists that have lost their bearing and their way, that Karate has a Way. It is the Way of Peace. Without the pursuit of Peace, Karate would become a brute activity for the purpose of hurting others. Since Karate was founded on the principles of peace, the

SHINZEN KARATE

most important value in Karate is that of preventing conflict. A Karateka is not a hammer made to smash others. A Karateka should pursue peace, in their personal life and in the Dojo. Defeating your opponent in confrontation is done with the purpose of creating peace. Peace is a pursuit and it is the highest ideal for a Karateka. Martial Artists should take heed that their students follow their words with respect and therefore the promotion of peace should become their most important goal. If peace is not the highest goal and winning at all costs is the highest goal, is that not self-defeating? Winning is establishing peace and establishing balance through the practice of Karate. Winning is preventing conflict and preventing confrontation before it manifests itself. Once the confrontation has started the prevention of escalation and the promotion of peace should be the highest goal.

Best Wishes,

Kambiz Mostofizadeh

SHINZEN KARATE

CHAPTER ONE – THE HISTORY OF KARATE

The history of karate is traced back to the Ryukyu Islands, of which Okinawa is the largest island. The earliest recognized date that the Ryukyu Kingdom started is widely disputed, however there is some evidence that places it in the 14th century. The capital of the Ryukyu Kingdom was Shuri, from which its inhabitants created the style of Shuri-te. Two other styles, Naha-te and Tomari-te, were also practiced in Naha and Tomari. With the coming of the Meiji Restoration in Japan in 1868 and plans by the ruling administration for rapid modernization, Karate was made available to the public. The Ryukyu Islands consisted of 55 islands positioned between Japan and China, and therefore were always in danger of occupation by both the Chinese and Japanese.   The Ryukyu Kingdom shared strong economic ties and held a tributary relationship with Chinese Authorities

SHINZEN KARATE

up until 1879. The Satsuma Clan conquered Okinawa in 1609 and forbid the use of weapons. This weapons ban caused Karate to be practiced more frequently and it pushed the creation of natural weapons that could be hidden from authorities. The lack of availability of weapons and the inability for commoners to afford weapons, meant that Ryukyu Islands residents were under constant danger. Many farming weapons were improvised to be used as weapons such as the sickle, nunchaku, and tonfa. The sickle meant to cut grain, nunchaku which was two pieces of wood connected by a leather strip used for beating rice, and the tonfa which was the handle of the hand operated rice mill became deadly weapons in the hand of a trained farmer. The meaning of kara is empty and te means hand. Its original translation was that of "Chinese Hand" because of the Chinese roots which Karate contains. Karate is the art of defending oneself without the use of weapons, only

SHINZEN KARATE

using hands and feet. The cultural, economic, and political ambassadors from China were rumored to have brought Chuan Fa or Shaolin Kung Fu to Okinawa. The use of techniques, such as the wrist lock in self defense maneuvers of karate, point to the stylistic origins tracing back to Kung Fu, which itself featured 36 grappling techniques. Sokon Matsumura (1797-1889), a student of a Chinese official in Okinawa, is widely recognized as the grandmaster of Karate because he taught Anko Itosu. Anko Itosu (1832-1915), a government official, taught Shuri-te karate and the Pinan katas to Gichin Funakoshi. The meaning of Anko is horse, and was a nickname used in place of Itosu's first name. Anko Itosu was given this nickname because he purportedly walked in a horse stance for hours on end. Funakoshi, a student of Itosu's Shuri-te, gave a demonstration of the prowess of Shuri-te to the Emperor of Japan and the Ministry of Education. Funakoshi proceeded to write

SHINZEN KARATE

and publish a manual in 1922 titled Ryukyu Kempo, which introduced the Okinawa martial arts system of Shuri-te to the public. Funakoshi re-branded Shuri-te as Shotokan Karate. Shoto meaning "pine-waves", which symbolized the sound of the wind as it blew through trees in the forest. Kan meaning hall or school, was the place that karate was practiced. Funakoshi adopted the belt system that had been created by Jigoro Kano, the founder of Judo. Funakoshi, an educator, taught Tokyo University Students and established the first university based Karate Club in Keio University, with the purpose of attracting students to promote karate. Funakoshi stressed the application of kata and insisted that two to three years be spent minimum on mastering each kata. There were many detractors who claimed there was too much focus on pre-defined sets of movements by Funakoshi. The Japanese government sponsored Funakoshi's Shotokan Karate and adopted it for military training. Despite the

SHINZEN KARATE

combat applications of Karate, Funakoshi emphasized the development of character and did not believe in the competitive tradition that has currently engulfed martial arts. Gichin Funakoshi is widely recognized by most martial arts scholars, as the father of modern karate. Kyokushin Karate is the second most popular form of Karate with over fifteen million practitioners worldwide. Kyokushin was started by Masutatsu Oyama, a southern Korean living in Japan, that held a 4th Dan Black Belt in Shotokan Karate and Judo. Mas Oyama, as he was called, had the reputation of a bushido warrior and a spiritualist. When Mas was 23 years old, he left civilization for Mt. Minobu, a forested mountain overlooking the Pacific Ocean. Mas spent over a year in solitude, pushing his mind and body to its limits. Mas punched trees in place of using a Makiwara (Ma-key-wa-ra) or wooden striking post. He would put himself through rigorous conditioning such as training within ice cold temperature waterfalls and

SHINZEN KARATE

breaking stones with his hands. After leaving Mt. Minobu, Mas competed in a karate championship, taking first place thereby propelling him to popularity. Mas immediately after his victory, opened his first Kyokushin Karate school in Tokyo on an empty lot. His school quickly grew to over 700 students, even with the high rate of students leaving from the hard conditioning. Mas invented the 100 man Kumite, where he would spar 100 people individually, one after another. Mas held this competition over 3 days, fighting 100 people each day. Competitors would fight until knocked out and injuries were not uncommon. The focus and use of effective techniques, made Mas Oyama's Kyokushin Karate, wildly popular. Mas was a fan of "one strike, one kill", believing that one powerful well placed strike is all that is needed to defeat an opponent. He certainly had trained his body to extreme heights, and his fighting experiences validated his belief. Kyokushin Karate

SHINZEN KARATE

arrived in the United Stated by way of
Hawaii in the early 1950's. Kyokyshin
Karate also spread throughout most of the
world, spurring on the popularization of
Karate. Karate tournaments became a
regular event throughout the United States,
Europe, and Asia. Karate spread for two
reasons; one being the popularization of
Karate via movies and secondly the
popularization came about via tournaments
where spectators watched live action.
Karate's fast pace nature and action style
made audiences flock to watch it. In the
1980's in the United States, Karate was
developing a large following and had
become America's most popular combat
sport.

SHINZEN KARATE

CHAPTER TWO – THE KARATE MINDSET

TEN RULES OF THE SHINZEN KARATE FIGHTING METHOD

Do Not Show Weakness To Your Enemy

The Best Defense Is More Offense

Do Not Strike First

Practice Constantly

Never Give Up

Be Fluid in Combat

Attack In Combination

Tae Sabaki (Constant Circling)

Courage

Hard & Soft Techniques

Rule 1 – Do Not Show Weakness To Your Enemy

SHINZEN KARATE

In the street or in competition, your enemy will seek to take advantage of your weakness. If you are hurt in a certain area, the opponent may seek to put even greater pressure in order to cause your defeat. The first rule is to not show weakness. We all have weakness, self-inflicted or other, but disguising them is key. Your opponent is most likely also hiding their pain in a fight or else they would give away an area that you can manipulate to your advantage. It is easy to get hurt in competition, in training, or on the street, which is why you should avoid revealing the pain that may exist. The Shinzen Karate method is about Strength and you must be strong on the inside as well as the outside in order to be a complete Karateka. All Karate fighters get bruises and have felt pain. The ability to bear blows from an opponent is what separates a Karateka from the average individual. Strength in offensive maneuvers as well as strength in defensive maneuvers are essential to a well balanced fighting

SHINZEN KARATE

style. Every block is an attack and every attack is defense. The Shinzen Karate method is first and foremost about developing strength in a student so that they will be strong enough to defeat opponents larger and more muscled than them.

Rule 2 – The Best Defense Is More Offense

If you are being attacked, you may be able to fend off the attacker with a few blocks, but you will not cause the attacker to back or retreat. Only so many strikes can be defended against until you have to attack. Attacking pushes the opponent back and causes them to retreat. There is no instance of a fight being won by purely defensive maneuvers. It is offensive maneuvers that win a fight. In order to win on the street or in a competition, you have to take the fight to the opponent. You have to back the opponent up by attacking them or else they will keep pushing forward. Defense is good for preventing an opponent from striking you but you must counter the opponent's strike with your own strike or else the opponent will continue striking you. Blocking techniques are an essential part of Shinzen Karate training but defense is just one half of the equation. Without a strong defense you cannot have a strong offense. You have to be able to block the opponent's strikes. More importantly than stopping their attacks, you are stopping their momentum as well as creating an opening for you to strike your opponent from. Thousands of hours should be spent perfecting the blocking methods of Shinzen Karate and this will give the student the self-confidence so that they can defend against an attack.

Rule 3 – Do Not Strike First

Karate Ni Sente Nashi which means that there is no first strike in Karate. Karate is an art of self-defense not an art of combat. Soldiers are students of combat but Karate practitioners or Karateka are students of

SHINZEN KARATE

self-defense. Karate is not a bully art. Karate is an art of peace and defense. All too often, the random violent act breaks out from road rage. A man exits his car and punches another man for driving too slow or too fast. It is a criminal act to assault another individual but people do it often and get away with it. You may have the luck of being assaulted on a Friday night at a party or a nightclub. You have to be able to show enough self-control to de-escalate a situation by just defending against wild strikes from drunken opponents. If you strike first, you will have escalated the situation, creating even more problems than had existed. The point of not striking first is so that you take the opportunity to deflate the pressure and tension in that situation. A Karateka is more concerned with peace and defense than attempting to start a fight. A Karateka would see no need to fight at all and this would give the Karateka the motive to attempt to stop a

SHINZEN KARATE

fight before it happens. Shinzen Karate is a style of self-defense and peace.

Rule 4 – Practice Constantly

There are too many overweight Black Belts walking around from bogus styles with Japanese sounding names. Maybe authenticity is growing thin because Karateka are not adhering to the most important rule in Karate and that is practice constantly. If you are thinking that you are not training enough then you are probably correct. You should be training at least 3 days and sometimes up to 5 days a week. Shinzen Karate is not about secret techniques or secret fighting methods. Shinzen Karate is about practicing constantly. The founder of Kyokushin Karate, Sosai Masutatsu Oyama, stressed constant training and regular practice. Oyama stated that an individual will reach mastery in Karate after 10,000 days of training Karate. No one has ever reached mastery by a few sessions of training.

SHINZEN KARATE

Karate training is a lifelong journey that must be embraced for what it is, a journey. All journeys take time so the student has time to experience varying levels of progress.

Rule 5 – Never Give Up

A fight is really a contest of wills. Your will has to be stronger than your opponent or the likely that you will lose is very high. A strong will allows you to achieve things you had not seemed possible. Having a strong will means being flexible in the face of difficulty. Never giving up means mentally preparing yourself to never accept defeat. You are not defeated when you lose, you are defeated when you quit. This is why you should have the fortitude to withstand difficulties and to never quit in the face of the opponent. If you are frightened, so is your opponent. Being strong in the face of opposition makes your opponent retreat. Having the will to endure the attacks of the opponent while looking for an opening to

SHINZEN KARATE

exploit to your advantage is part of the Shinzen Karate method. Shinzen Karate is a power style of Karate and power must meet power head on. It is advancement in the face of difficulty and refusing to retreat when facing the opposition. The Shinzen Karate method is about never giving up.

Rule 6 – Be Fluid In Combat

Fluidity in combat depends on movement and maneuvering. The point of fluidity is to prevent the opponent from landing a strike and to be able to maneuver in to a position where you can strike the opponent with ease without them being able to strike you. The opponent will try to find your opening and to exploit it with an attack. If you are constantly moving your head and your hips in a way which prevents the opponent from targeting an opening, then your opponent will be unable to strike you with any degree of effectiveness. Your movement will prevent the enemy striking you because your head and body will have moved out of

SHINZEN KARATE

the range of the attacks of the opponent. The second part of being fluid in combat is maneuvering your body to a position where you can easily strike your opponent without them being able to strike you. As a Karateka, in a fight, you should not get hit at all. Your defensive training of blocking and sliding under punches or kicks will prepare you to maintain an effective defensive posture. The Shinzen Karate method of fighting depends on fluidity in movement so as to evade the opponent's strikes while positioning oneself to strike the opponent with ease.

Rule 7 – Attack In Combination

The Shinzen Karate method of fighting depends on the Karateka launching attacks in combination. Punches, blocks, sweeps, and kicks are put together in combination. Even if one strike fails to land there will be more strikes in combination targeting the opponent making their defense untenable. Combinations are used to confuse the

SHINZEN KARATE

opponent and to disrupt the opponent's defensive posture. They may block one or two strikes but they will be unable to block 4 or 5 strikes in rapid combination. Because the Shinzen Karate method depends on attacks in combination, the Karateka must make great effort to practice punches, kicks, sweeps, and blocks in combination so they will be usable in a real situation. Karateka should attempt to practice with multiple opponents so as to train their mind and body to fight various sizes of people. The Karateka should also have multiple fighters attack them simultaneously to train the mind to fight multiple opponents. Attacks in combination should be practiced in real time sparring so the Karateka get real time experience applying the attacks in combination. Karateka can also practice attacks in combination on a heavy bag. The Shinzen Karate method of attacks in combination are proven to be more effective than single strike attacks. The opponent becomes confused and is unable

SHINZEN KARATE

to defend against multiple attacks simultaneously, causing their defense to open further, immediately making them vulnerable to your striking.

Rule 8 – Tae Sabaki

The Tae Sabaki method is an essential part of the Shinzen Karate fighting method. The Tae Sabaki method is to constantly circle around your opponent's weak side (jab), making them off-balance and unable to throw power strikes with effectiveness. An off-balance fighter cannot throw power strikes because they have no base (both of their feet are not on the floor). Since power for a strike is derived from the ground up, a fighter without both feet on the floor will be unable to deliver a strike with any force behind it. The Shinzen Karate method of fighting incorporates the highly effective method of Tae Sabaki. By constantly circling, you do not provide a stable target for your opponent's attacks. Your opponent can also get tangled up in your body's circling if they launch an attack while you are circling. Tae Sabaki is a key part of the Karateka's style because it naturally prevents the opponent from having a stable base to strike from and it prevents the opponent from being able to accurately gauge the distance and timing to be able to strike you.

Rule 9 – Courage

You can't attack if you are scared of being hit. You have to have courage in the face of the opponent. If you are scared then you should not let it show. Your opponent is not some supernatural being with superpowers. Your opponent is a human just like you. If you are scared, then so is your opponent. Courage means standing in the face of the opponent and being victorious. It is difficult to have courage and it is easy to be a coward. Courage has to be built up in your heart and you should never have fear in the face of your opponent. There could be a situation where you are with your family

SHINZEN KARATE

and a stranger threatens you in a park. Courage is for such a time. Or when you are in your home and you think there could be a burglar on your front porch. Courage is needed at this very time. Courage should not make you cruel or mean. Courage should make you strong in the face of an opponent or an enemy. There are many instances of great Martial Artists and all of them were courageous and brave. None of them were cowards. None of them. It was courage that made them victorious in the face of various obstacles and difficulties. Courage makes the difference between a win and a loss. The Shinzen Karate method of fighting depends on having courage and being courageous in the face of your opponent.

Rule 10 – Hard & Soft Techniques

The Shinzen Karate method of fighting incorporates both hard and soft techniques. Hard techniques are punches, kicks, elbow strikes, and knees strikes. Soft techniques

SHINZEN KARATE

are sweeps, throws, trips, and simple submission techniques. When Kung Fu was imported from China to Japan, the original name for the Shaolin school of Kung Fu was Kem-po, a direct pronunciation of the words Chuan Fa (Kung Fu). The 108 submission techniques of Chin-na were passed on to Karate practitioners. Varying styles including Omari-te, Naha-te, and Shuri-te were later developments influenced by the original Kempo. If multiple attackers attack you, you have to be able to buy time between each attacker in order to have a successful chance of surviving. The first attacker may attempt to punch you, only to have his shoulder locked in submission while you front kick the second attacker. The combination of hard (striking) and soft (submissions and throws) will have to be used by you for surviving against multiple attackers. Since the ground on the street is concrete, rough, and incongruent, it would be most dangerous to attempt to grapple on the concrete floor.

SHINZEN KARATE

Concrete is not soft and pliant like the tatami in a Dojo. Concrete hurts and it can kill a person if they hit it hard enough. This is why you should never wrestle or grapple on concrete floor in a fight. If you fall, your first priority should be to stand up as fast as possible. You will be taken down only if you are not aware. You will be taken down and held down only if you want to be held down. Against multiple attackers, it would be most dangerous to grapple on the ground in a fight because one of them may kick your head on the ground, causing you permanent damage. Your priority should be to stand and use both hard and soft techniques in fluid combination to ward off the attackers. In order to do so, you must have some level of experience beforehand in fighting with hard and soft techniques. Gichin Funakoshi, the founder of Shotokan Karate laid out his own set of principles of Karate.

SHINZEN KARATE

Respect & Courtesy
Gichin Funakoshi believed that respect and courtesy are the basis of martial arts. Funakoshi taught that the practice of karate started with the showing of respect and courtesy by acknowledging your opponent or training partner by bowing to them.

No First Attack
Karate practitioners are taught to never attack first, unless the karate practitioner is witnessing an incident and to not use the martial arts to defend the victim would be an injustice. Karate is a self defense art that's to be used for protecting your body and that of your loved ones.

Use of Karate for the cause of Justice
Karate practitioners are only authorized to use their martial skills in order to uphold justice.

SHINZEN KARATE

Self-Examination
Funakoshi taught that it's vital to practice self-examination and understand your strengths and weaknesses before understanding the strengths and weaknesses of others.

The Spirit over Techniques
For Funakoshi, competition and the effectiveness of techniques were not as important as the "spirit" in which the techniques were practiced. By spirit, Funakoshi meant the nature in which the techniques were practiced. The nature that Funakoshi wished the karate practitioner to practice was, that of concentration, devotion, purity of intention, and an attitude that aimed for character development.

Complete Immersion
Funakoshi taught that to fully immerse oneself into karate, was the way to true understanding of karate's applications. The

SHINZEN KARATE

movements of karate practitioners in combat was conditioned by Funakoshi's demand of the repetitive practice of Kata. The training of the body, conditioned the body to move in ways that had been previously practiced by way of pre-defined movements.

Safety Is Derived from Careful Attention

The lack of attention that is paid to safety by some karate practitioners has resulted in many injuries, minor and life threatening. Safety depends on constant attention during training so as to not injure yourself and/or your opponent.

Karate Is Not Limited to the Training Hall

Karate as a system of self-defense and an effective martial art, depends on the practitioners to be able to practice not only within the training hall, but also outside. The training hall provides the proper environment for the learning and growth of

SHINZEN KARATE

the vital principles and techniques that comprise karate, however, it is the supplemental training conducted that allows rapid progress. Two hours spent outside the training hall is sufficient for a practitioner to master the techniques first learned within the training hall or Dojo.

Karate is a Lifelong Journey
It is the belief of many practitioners that karate's techniques can just be learned and mastered without the thousands of hours that mastery demands. Karate is a lifelong journey, and every student, regardless of their ranking, will not stop being a student. To believe otherwise, would be disadvantageous because the practitioner would feel content with what they have already learned, thereby limiting their growth. The culmination of the experiences of karate practitioners, provide the base for further technical proficiency.

SHINZEN KARATE

Karate's Secrets are in Living the Way
There are secrets within the movements
and techniques of karate, that can be only
be discovered by constantly living the way
of karate. The principles of karate define
the way, and the practitioners are
the vehicles for living the way.

Constant Practice Maintains Your Skill
It is natural for karate practitioners to take
time off from training to rest their bodies
and minds, but to neglect training will not
only result in halting growth in martial skill,
but also can have the negative effect of
decreasing practitioners access to muscle
memory.

Do Not Fall Behind
It is concerning for a karate teacher, to
witness a student that is overly obsessed
with winning. Obsession with
competitiveness is frowned upon

SHINZEN KARATE

because it causes frictions that generate rivalries sometimes resulting in unintended consequences.

Victory Depends on Recognizing Gaps

In order to defeat the opponent and achieve victory, it is important to recognize the vulnerabilities or gaps of the opponent. The vulnerabilities are gaps left undefended by the opponent.

Outcome of Battle is Decided by Knowledge

The outcome of a battle is decided by the parties knowledge of their own weaknesses and strengths.

Keep Your Defenses Prepared

Evasions. feints, blocks and/or movements should be used to deny an opponent's strikes from being effective. Think of the opponent's feet and hands as weapons that should be avoided at all costs.

SHINZEN KARATE

Keep Constant Awareness

It cannot be predicted when a potential attack will materialize. Your enemies may be working against you actively to ruin or destroy you in one shape or another. Constant awareness protects its practitioner from inactivity which carelessness creates. Always be aware of your surroundings because attacks can happen when least expected. When encountering an adversary or opponent, understanding their movements, could be advantageous to you in a conflict.

Posture Mastery is Vital

It is very important for beginning practitioners of karate, to constantly practice and master the postures. The use of the horse stance and lower stances in general, should be mastered by beginners. As the student progresses to an advanced level, the use of a natural and erect posture should be adopted.

SHINZEN KARATE

Kata Mastery is Not Combat Mastery

Kata stimulates blood circulation, prepares the body for increasing training intensity, trains the muscle memory, conditions the practitioners postures, and teaches techniques that contain the secrets to self defense. Despite these benefits, it is important to understand that mastery of Kata, is not the master of combat. Although the Katas contain the applications of combat, the pre-defined movements of the Kata are practiced in the absence of an opponent, that would simulate the realities which materialize in combat.

Know Your Limits

Constantly gauge your skills levels on multiple levels including your agility, stamina, flexibility, postures, punching, kicking, blocking, and others. Know your limitations and use this knowledge to assist your training.

SHINZEN KARATE

Constant Improvement
Continuously work to improve yourself by conditioning your body and improving your mind.

CHAPTER THREE – KARATE TECHNIQUES

Before beginning training, it is essential to properly "warm-up" your muscles so as to prevent injuries. Many karate practitioners use kata to "warm-up", but it is essential to recognize that stretching is the foundation for training. Stretching regularly maintains the flexibility and health of its practitioner. The use of kata and stretching in pre-defined sets are similar because both promote the circulation of blood, thereby bestowing health benefits. The karate practitioner should start with warming up the neck and shoulder muscles, arms, elbows, wrists, fingers, waist, groin muscles, hamstring muscles, calves, knees, and ankles. Stretching should be done in a

SHINZEN KARATE

natural manner without pressuring the body, ultimately causing you pain and injury. The stretching period should last no less than 15 minutes and no longer 30 minutes. The stretching period not only warms the muscles, but also is a meditative like exercise that mentally prepares the practitioner's mind. Stretching will reduce the injuries sustained during training and has the effect of increasing practitioners ability to perform at a higher pace. When stretching, use caution so as to not stretch the muscle or muscles to the point that you feel pain. Do not bounce when stretching the muscle, and also hold an even level of tension while stretching in a stationary form or pose. Incorporate isometric stretching using a wall or a stationary barrier to generate tension on the muscles. Isometric stretching, as a type of static stretching, includes the use of wall push-ups. Stretching is vital to the karate practitioner and is the basis for the start of every training session.

SHINZEN KARATE

HARD TECHNIQUES

Roundhouse Kick (Mawashi Geri)

Front Kick (Mae Geri)

Side Kick (Yoko Geri)

Back Kick (Ushiro Geri)

Axe Kick (Ono Geri)

Crescent Kick (Mikazuki Geri)

Spinning Hook Kick (Ushiro Mawashi Geri)

Knee Strike (Hiza Geri)

Jumping Knee (Tobi Hiza Geri)

Jab (Kizame Tsuki)

Reverse Punch (Gyaku Tsuki)

Jumping Reverse Punch (Tobi Gyaku Tsuki)

Spinning Back Fist (Ushiro Uriken)

SHINZEN KARATE

Elbow Strike (Empi Uchi)

Jumping Elbow Strike (Tobi Empi Uchi)

Spinning Elbow Strike (Ushiro Empi Uchi)

Palm Strike (Teisho Tsuki)

Kicking Levels

Low Kick – Gedan. Below the waist is considered the Gedan area.

Mid Kick – Chudan. From the neck to the waist is considered Chudan area.

High Kick – Jodan. From the neck up is considered Jodan.

Most kicking techniques can be applied to the three areas of Gedan, Chudan, and Jodan. It is important to target areas before striking for better accuracy. As previously stated, most of the following kicking techniques can be applied to the Gedan target area, Chudan target area, and Jodan target area.

SHINZEN KARATE

Jodan is obviously a harder target to strike than chudan or gedan, and that is becaue the opponent can move their head away from a strike while their chudan or gedan may still be in striking range.

TARGET AREAS

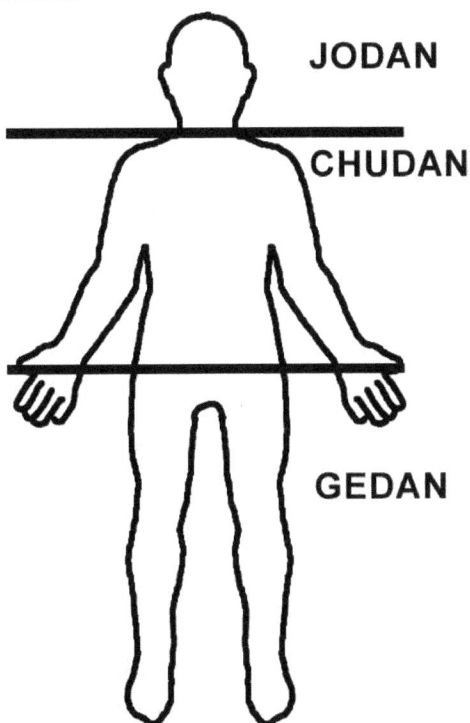

JODAN

CHUDAN

GEDAN

Chudan strikes are easier to achieve simply

SHINZEN KARATE

because the target area of the chudan is larger than the jodan. The jodan area and gedan areas are smaller than the chudan making them naturally more difficult to strike in contrast to the chudan. A Reverse Punch aimed at the chudan area of the opponent will have greater accuracy. The gedan area of the opponent may be the first to come in to your striking range and will provide you the first opportunity to strike your opponent. If you are able to strike the gedan area effectively, this will slow your opponent down and will cause their kicking techniques to become weaker. If the opponent is stronger than you, focus on attacking their chudan area's core (abdomen) to take their power away. Use the target areas as a guide for your techniques and call out the target area in your mind before launching the technique in order to be sure of the target area you will be attacking. Kicking techniques are not thrown for the sake of kicking. Your accuracy and your strength will determine to what extent the opponent will be impacted. Kicking should be executed in perfect form with the leg kept loose and nimble during delivery. The looser the leg is kept, the faster the delivery of the kick. A tightened up leg slows down the technique. Kicking is an art onto itself that should be practiced with consistency and lucidity of awareness. The more hours your spend kicking and honing your kicking skills, the greater proficiency you will develop while perfecting your kicking form and delivery.

Roundhouse Kick

The most important kicking technique in Shinzen Karate is the roundhouse kick. The roundhouse kick generates immense strength from the hips with the kick striking the opponent's leg quad muscles with powerful force. An opponent can be knocked down or incapacitated with powerful roundhouse kicks. In the sport of Muay Thai, roundhouse kicks slice upwards in to the opponent's body. In the sport of

SHINZEN KARATE

Karate, roundhouse kicks slice downwards in to the opponent's quad muscles. This allows for greater momentum and strength in roundhouse kicks. The roundhouse kick is the most dependable kick in a confrontation and it is a kick that is difficult to block against if thrown low at the opponent's quad muscles. The analogy is that of a baseball bat slamming in to your legs at 120 kilometers per hour. Tens of thousands of hours should be spent on this most important technique and its technical refinement should be taken seriously. The power of the roundhouse kick is generated by the hips and waist of the Karateka. The roundhouse kick can be aimed at the opponent's quad muscles, stomach, chest, or face. It is seemingly the easiest kick to learn but among the most difficult to master. A Black Belt in Karate should have the ability to deliver the roundhouse kick with ease to various areas of the opponent while maintaining perfect balance and form.

SHINZEN KARATE

Front Kick

The front kick is the most direct kick with the highest probability of landing on the opponent. This is because the front kick is direct and delivered in a straight line. The shortest point between A and Z is a straight line and the front kick can deliver an immense amount of force to the stomach or chest of an opponent. The front kick can also be delivered to the front leg of an opponent to incapacitate them. The Shinzen Karate method of fighting depends

SHINZEN KARATE

on being able to deal with opponents quickly and easily. If you are attacked by multiple opponents, the front kick can help to buy you time by creating time and space between yourself and your opponents. It is essential to raise your knee to the highest level possible to generate the maximum amount of force before you extend your leg to strike the opponent. The higher you raise your knee, the greater the force that will be generated. The front kick is a highly effective kick that knock the wind out of your opponent or the front kick can be used in a jabbing manner to gauge the distance between yourself and the opponent. The jumping front kick can also generate immense force because the entire weight of your body is directed behind the kick. In a confrontation, the front kick will back up your opponent and cause them to re-consider attacking you. The front kick has proven its effectiveness in street fighting and in competition, because it is a direct and straightforward striking technique that

SHINZEN KARATE

has a high probability of landing on the opponent. The Shinzen Karate method of fighting depends on using techniques that are efficient, effective, and direct and the Front Kick is unique in containing all three qualities.

Side Kick

The side kick is a very effective kick that can cause the opponent to back up and to become off-balance in attempting to evade it. The side kick, if properly applied, can throw an opponent back many meters or it can knockout an opponent if landed to the face or stomach of the opponent. The side kick's rapid delivery makes it a difficult kick to defend against. The Karateka's rapid forward body movement when delivering the side kick is able to overwhelm the opponent and cause them to make a mistake. The side kick generates great strength in its delivery giving the Karateka a formidable weapon for dealing with an attacker. The side kick, although seemingly simple, has the advantage of being able to catch the opponent off-guard.

The Back Kick

The Shinzen Karate method of fighting depends on being able to strike your opponent without your opponent being able to strike you back. The back kick is an excellent kick for creating time and space between yourself and the opponent. The back kick can be used to jab your opponent or it can be used to push your opponent away. The back kick, because of the strength of the hips and waist, is able to generate an immense amount of power. The back kick can be aimed at the legs, stomach, chest, or face of the opponent. The back kick requires the Karateka to turn to deliver the back kick. The turning of the Karateka generates power from the hips and waist. Many opponents have been knocked out or knocked down from a powerful back kick delivered directly to an opponent's abdomen. The back kick is one of the most powerful techniques in the arsenal of a Karateka but it is not an easy technique to master. If applied incorrectly, the Karateka can be thrown off balance or worse thrown on the ground. The back kick is a main tool for the Shinzen Karate practitioner and it should be practiced constantly to achieve perfect form and control.

The Axe Kick

The Axe Kick is a very powerful and useful technique from long and close range. The

SHINZEN KARATE

axe kick is delivered by the Karateka raising one leg to the maximum elevation and then slamming that leg on to the head or shoulder of the opponent.

Late Kyokushin legend Andy Hug used the axe kick regularly to destroy his opponents in K1 competition. The axe kick can be used to knock out an opponent or to damage their shoulder, making their ability to counter both slower and weaker. The higher the leg is lifted up before it is brought down on to the opponent, the greater the level of force that will be generated. The axe kick must be mastered and practiced extensively before use because a sloppy axe kick can result in the Karateka falling. An axe kick is seemingly ease to use but very difficult to master. Hitting a stationary heavy bag with an axe kick is much different than landing an axe kick on a moving target. This is why the axe kick should only be used when a high level of proficiency has been achieved.

Crescent Kick

The Crescent Kick is a favorite among the Shinzen Karate techniques used. The crescent kick is fast, efficient, powerful, and versatile. The crescent kick can be delivered from the outside in or from the inside out. The crescent kick's speed is able to surprise an opponent as well as to off-balance an opponent. The crescent kick is difficult to defend against and it is delivered in a circular (crescent like) motion. The nature of the crescent kick makes it a difficult technique to master and an even more difficult kick to counter. The crescent kick can also be delivered from mid range to close range without putting the Karateka in harm's way. The Shinzen Karate method of fighting favors the powerful and fast speed crescent kick because of its ability to surprise the opponent.

Spinning Hook Kick

The spinning hook kick is in effect a reverse roundhouse kick. The spinning of the body and the centrifical force generated powers the spinning hook kick. It is a very strong kick because of the spinning of the body. The spinning hook kick like the crescent kick, is fast, powerful, and also has a surprising element to it. Timing and distance must be perfectly gauged so as to increase the probability that the kick will be successful. Proper form and execution of the technique depends on constant practice. Once form and execution of the technique have been mastered, the student can turn towards achieving timing and proper distance for the spinning hook kick to be effective. The spinning hook kick is an advanced technique that requires tens of thousands of hours to be mastered but once mastered is an extremely effective weapon.

Front Knee Strike

The front knee strike can knock the wind out of an opponent or can hurt them so as to prevent them from continuing the fight. A front knee strike, when delivered to the ribs, will slow down or completely stop an opponent from fighting back. It can cause immense pain in the opponent's ribs making it difficult for them to breath. The front knee kick should be practiced in the clinch on a live opponent in real time sparring or it should be practiced on a heavy bag.

SHINZEN KARATE

Jumping Knee

The jumping knee is a very powerful technique because the entire weight of the Karateka is put in to it. If the jumping knee lands to an opponent's face, they will be knocked out instantly or at the least stunned. The jumping knee also helps to put the Karateka in to a position where they are closer to their opponent. The jumping knee can be delivered from close range or mid range, launching the Karateka up and forward in to the opponent with the area of impact being the front and top of the knee. The jumping knee is a main technique for Shinzen Karate practitioners and it is highly valued for its ability to knockout opponents with immense force.

Foot Sweep

The Foot Sweep or Gedan Barai is one of the most basic techniques in Karate. It is an effective technique that is used from close range to make the opponent drop to the floor with minimal strength used. The application of leverage is used to drop the opponent to the floor. This technique, like all techniques in Karate, requires study and practice in order for the student to develop a sufficient enough level of proficiency. In order to do so, this technique like all techniques in Karate, should be practiced in real time.

PUNCHES

Karate's punching techniques are fast, strong, effective, and efficient. The use of straight line attacks in punching techniques generate a significant amount of power because the strength is generated by the rotation of the practitioner's hips. While standing in Zenkutsu Datchi or front stance with the left leg in front and right leg in back, the left hand is held up and slightly forward for protecting the left side of the face, while the right hand is held up and slightly back to defend the right side of the face. In this formation, the left hand would

SHINZEN KARATE

be the jab hand and the right hand would be the reverse punch hand. The reverse punch generates a larger amount of force than the jab because the reverse punch travels a longer distance to its target. The reverse punch's greater length to striking its target, allows for greater rotation of the hips, thereby generating greater strength. Punches should be used in swift combinations for effectiveness and power should be generated from the hips, not from the shoulder or arm muscles. It is important to not tense the muscles when punching and to keep the neck and shoulders loose as possible. The arm should be kept as loose as possible until the very last moment of delivery. The punching arm's muscles should tense at the last moment of delivery to maximize strength and to not reduce your speed during the punch's delivery. The jab is faster than the reverse punch, has less power, but has the feature of allowing you to gauge the distance to your opponent. Maintaining a

SHINZEN KARATE

proper punching fist is also important because your knuckles are the first point of contact with your opponent. Many fists have been broken during training and sparring because the practitioners have not maintained the proper punching fist. The punching fist should be firmly clenched with the thumb covering over the index and middle finger.   The punching hand's wrist should not be bent upward or downward, but should be held in a straight posture. Due to the popularity of sports Karate, hook punches, uppercuts, and spinning back punches have been incorporated into the repertoire of techniques used during matches. Although punching is used less per ratio than kicks, punching techniques remain to be the base of a karate practitioner's arsenal. According to the Bubishi, the knife hand strike was able to cause unconsciousness, seizures, and temporary loss of speech in an opponent.

SHINZEN KARATE

Jab

The jab is the most basic and fundamental of the punching techniques in Shinzen Karate. The jab allows the Karateka to gauge the distance between themselves and the opponent. Once the jab has gauged the distance, the reverse punch (power punch) can be used to finish off the opponent. The jab is a fast and effective punch that is used to setup the reverse punch. The jab has two parts to it and they are the step and the strike. If you are standing in Zenkutsu Datchi (Front Stance) with your left leg forward and your right leg back, as you throw your jab step out with your left leg. This will increase your power by putting your bodily weight in to the punch, making for a stronger punch with a higher velocity. The secret to an effective jab is to understand the range and the weaknesses of the opponent. Jabbing finds the distance between yourself and the opponent but it also sets up your most

SHINZEN KARATE

important punch, the reverse punch. Use the jab to keep the opponent at a distance and use the jab to disrupt the defense of your opponent. The jab can be highly effective if used in a measured and calculated manner. The jab can knockout an incoming opponent using their own force to knock them out when they run in to your jab. The jab can be used in a forward leaping manner also to surprise the opponent and to disrupt their momentum.

Reverse Punch

SHINZEN KARATE

The reverse punch is the most powerful punch used by a Shinzen Karate practitioner. Once the lead jab has found the distance between you and the opponent, the reverse punch is used to attempt to knockout the opponent. The reverse punch delivers great force from the rotation of the hips and waist. The reverse punch is easy to learn but difficult to master. If you strike the opponent with a reverse punch and the opponent is unfazed and un-hurt, it is because you are not applying the reverse punch properly. Various exercises can be used to increase the strength of the reverse punch but the most important of them all is the handstand. The handstand exercise strengthens the core, shoulders, arms, and upper body of the Karateka, giving them a clear advantage over their opponents in punching. It is important to step your left leg forward during the delivery of your reverse punch. Doing so will increase the

SHINZEN KARATE

strength of your punch by putting your body weight in to it.

Jumping Reverse Punch

The Jumping Reverse Punch is a feint (false strike) with a jumping reverse punch. The Karateka throws a jab, dips low before the jump to increase their jumping height, and jumps up striking the opponent with a reverse punch while coming down. It is a surprise technique and one that can disrupt the momentum of an opponent.

SHINZEN KARATE

Spinning Back Fist

The spinning back fist is a powerful technique that is used to surprise an opponent and to break up their guard. The spinning back fist is able to surprise the opponent because they are not expecting it. It can be used to setup a roundhouse kick or a front kick. The spinning back fist can be used in a stationary manner or in a jumping manner. If it connects with the opponent, the likelihood that they could be knocked out is high. It is an effective and useful technique. The power is generated by turning movement of the hips.

The Elbow Strike

The elbow strike is a powerful strike that can be thrown to the face and head of the opponent. The elbow strike can be used in a stationary manner or in a jumping manner. The elbow strike is a knockout blow that can easily send an opponent to the ground. The elbow strike is used for self-defense

SHINZEN KARATE

purposes and is not practiced in real time sparring in the Dojo because of the pain that could be inflicted with one elbow strike. The elbow strike is practiced on a Heavy Bag for safe training. The variation of the elbow strike, the jumping elbow, is very useful in a street fight as well as competition because of its ability to inflict a maximum level of pain on your opponent.

Jumping Elbow Strike

The jumping elbow strike is very effective against taller opponents. It has a few advantages which make it a formidable technique against a bigger opponent. The first advantage is that it closes the gap between you and your opponent without allowing the opponent to strike you while entering their guard. The second advantage is that the jumping elbow strike put the opponent on the defensive, forcing them to protect their face and to back up. The third advantage is that it is a technique that can knockout your opponent if it lands. It is a very effective in the street and it will cause your opponent to be frightened and to back up.

Spinning Elbow Strike

The spinning elbow strike is a very effective technique for close range fighting. The Karateka throws a jab at the opponent with their left hand and spins around landing their right elbow on the opponent's face. The movement of the hips in spinning generate an immense amount of power that can knockout an opponent if the technique lands. If the technique does not land, the opponent will be forced to back in a defensive posture to prevent being hit.

The Palm Strike

The palm strike is a very effective open handed strike that is used to striking an opponent's chin or nose. The palm strike is a direct attack that is both and efficient. It is difficult to defend against because of its rapidity and straight line nature. It is a technique that is effective in the street for self-defense as well as being a technique that can stop a fight quickly. Use with caution in training and always use safety equipment to prevent injuries.

Training vs Fighting

Training on a heavy bag or training on a Makiwara prepares you to strike. A Heavy Bag does move but it probably will not move in a way that resembles a live attacking opponent. A Makiwara is an effective tool for developing power but the Makiwara does not move either. Training to fight can only be done with a live opponent that is attacking and defending in real time. This is the most realistic and effective way of training. For safety purposes the sparring training should be done with less power so as to prevent injuries to either party.

SHINZEN KARATE

CHAPTER FOUR – BLOCKING TECHNIQUES

The word "Uke" means "to receive" and therefore in Karate, each attack by an opponent is met by an "Uke" (the receiving of the opponent's energy).

Low Block (Gedan Barai Uke)

Inside Block (Soto Uke)

Outside Block (Uchi Uke)

Overhead Block (Jodan Age Uke)

These are the 4 Main Blocking Techniques in Shinzen Karate. Blocking a punch in real time depends on practicing to block a punch in real time. This could only be done in muted sparring (sparring with less power used). The more time you spend practicing punches in real time the greater proficiency you will develop in doing so.

SHINZEN KARATE

Low Block

The low block is the most basic block in
Shinzen Karate. The low block is effective
for stopping kicks and punches to your
abdomen. The fist of the low block should
start from behind your ear and come
downwards diagonally across your body.
This motion will generate a considerable
amount of power which will allow you to
deflect the opponent's strike with force.

SHINZEN KARATE

Inside Block

The Inside Block is an effective blocking technique for stopping a punch or kick to your chest and face. The fist of the inside block starts from the ear. For example, the right fist is held to the right ear with the right elbow out at a 45 degree angle. As the opponent's strike comes towards you, your right elbow is swung in towards your chest while your right fist is held tightly against your right ear. The greater force you use in turning your hips, the greater power you will generate when deflecting (blocking) the opponent's strike. It is important to start the inside block from your ear and to pull in to your elbow to generate greater strength.

Outside Block

The outside block (also called Roundhouse Block or Round Block) is an effective blocking technique for stopping an opponent's roundhouse kick. It is also effective for stopping a punch at your chest. The outward motion of the outside block generates sufficient enough strength to deflect the opponent's strike, causing them to move off-balance.

Overhead Block

The Overhead Block is effective for stopping an opponent's Axe Kick. It is also effective for deflecting an opponent's punch to your face. It is seemingly the easiest block to learn but among the most difficult blocks to master. The overhead block is an advanced technique that requires perfect speed and timing to stop an opponent's attack.

CHAPTER FIVE - TOOLS FOR TRAINING KARATE

Makiwara – The makiwara is a wooden striking post. It is the most simple of the tools in Karate but arguably the most effective. There are round Makiwaras and there are square Makiwaras. The Makiwara builds striking strength and power. It can be used as a kicking post as well as being punched. The Makiwara is usually covered with rope at the top to prevent damage to the hand.

Heavy Bag – The heavy bags should be at least 40 kilos in weight and it should be struck with power and speed. It is important to move around the heavy bag as

SHINZEN KARATE

if they are a real opponent. The most important rule is you will fight how you practice. The heavy bag should be one of the main tools that you use for training. The heavier the heavy bag, the greater power you will build by training it. Too heavy of a bag can slow down your technique. The ideal weight for a training heavy bag is between 40 to 100 kilos.

Karate Exercise Drills

Each Dojo has their own curriculum for how they operate and maintain a proper fitness program for optimum performance in Karate competition. This curriculum is unique to Shinzen Karate as well as sharing the same practices as styles such as Kyokushin.

One step sparring – 1) Opponent attacks you with reverse punch 2) You block incoming reverse punch with roundhouse block and step in with reverse punch.

SHINZEN KARATE

Two Step Sparring – 1) You attack with a reverse punch. 2) Opponent blocks your reverse punch with an outside block and delivers fronthand jab to your chest.

Three Step Sparring 1) You attack with reverse punch 2) Opponent blocks with your reverse punch with an overhead block and steps in with reverse punch 3) You block reverse punch with roundhouse block and step in with reverse punch.

100 Punch Drill – Stand in a horse stance and deliver 100 punches with timing, perfect form, and simultaneous breathing.

4 Direction Kick Drill – Standing in a Front Stance with your left leg forward. Deliver a Front Kick with your Right Leg, and then turn 45 degrees deliver a front kick with your right leg, and then turn 45 degrees deliver a front kick with your right leg, and then turn 45 degrees and deliver front kick with your right leg. Total of 4 kicks delivered, one in each direction.

SHINZEN KARATE

100 Steps All Fours Drill – Walk on all fours (on hands and feet) for 100 steps. This exercise develops your upper and body strength as well as strengthening your core.

100 Seconds High Knees Drill – Cardiovascular exercise for strengthening your heart and lungs as well as quads.

100 Blocks Drill – Execute 100 Blocking Techniques (Low Block, Roundhouse Block, Inside Block, Overhead Block) in sequence, doing 25 of each.

8 Direction Sparring Drill – The 8 Direction Sparring Drill has the Karateka attacking multiple imaginary opponents that are standing in the 8 directions surrounding the Karateka. This is a very effective drill for building awareness, honing techniques, as well as building stamina.

Note: All of the drills mentioned above are practical and applicable for preparing the Karateka in technique as well as building

SHINZEN KARATE

their fitness level. The Drills should be used in sequence or used in alternation.

KATA

Gichin Funakoshi of Shotokan Karate stressed the use of Kata and stated that Kata contained all the secrets within Karate. Each style of Karate has its own Kata and its own nuances in stances and techniques. Shinzen Karate has a limited amount of Katas and that is because its focus is on actual fighting. Still there are various Katas that are performed in Shinzen Karate and they are useful for concentration and focus. Breathing is most important during the performance of Kata and it is important to speed up and slow down during the performance of various parts of the Kata. Kata also has the added benefit of being able to instill balance in its practitioner. Balance is the most important element of a Karate practitioner. Without balance, the opponent can easily knock you down. Kata trains the Karate practitioner in balance as

SHINZEN KARATE

well as focus and concentration. Memorizing each Kata takes time but their automatic performance can be realized through repeated training in each Kata. Kata is a word that is comprised of three words; "katachi" which mean shape, "kai" which means cut, and "tsuchi" which means the earth or ground. A kata is a pre-defined set of movements that are practiced at various speeds to instill "muscle memory" in its practitioners. The mastery of a kata allows the practitioner to be able to repeat the moves at will without thinking. The sequential flow of blocks, punches, kicks, evasions, and movements contain elements which can be used in real combat. The creators of kata are disputed, but it is a fact that it was Gichin Funakoshi that brought the practice of kata to the mainstream. Funakoshi's insistence on repeated diligent practice in the movements of kata, took precedence over the practice of sparring. Mas Oyama, the founder of Kyokushin

SHINZEN KARATE

Karate, stressed the three fundamentals for the practice of kata as:

Waza no Kankyu – Tempo
The speed of techniques used should vary depending on the movements. Some techniques should be executed slowly and some should be performed quickly.

Chikara no Kyojaku – Force
The force used should be even with a balance between strength and balance throughout, with the practitioner pacing themselves until the moment of delivery of each strike or block.

Iki no Chosei – Breath Control
Breath control and the regulation of breathing is vital so as the practitioner can perform for longer periods of time.

Oyama believed that the movements of kata trained the karate practicioner for combat in contrast to Funakoshi that

SHINZEN KARATE

believed kata is not combat. Oyama however used the movements in real time and insisted on live sparring in contrast to Funakoshi which forbade sparring. The eventual split in Karate was between two camps; Kyokushin which focused on sparring, and Shotokan which focused on kata.

CHAPTER SIX - CRITICS OF KARATE

The critics of Karate come from various styles and various backgrounds. Each of them believes their own style to be better than every other style and each of them believes that Karate is not applicable in this modern age of cage and octagonal ring fighting. So who are the first critics of Karate? Fake martial artists that never earned a Black Belt in any style are quick to speak ill about Karate. Karate training, for those that have not experienced the inside of an authentic Karate dojo, is hard training. Hard on the mind, hard on the body, and

SHINZEN KARATE

hard on the spirit. This is why Karate Black Belts have such strong wills against bigger and sometimes stronger opponents. They have been trained to never quit in the Dojo, no matter what they odds are against and how powerful their opponent claims to be. Karateka accept only thing in regards to an opponent they are facing, either that opponent is going to knock me out or I am going to knock them out. If the opponent of a Karateka is lucky enough to knockout the Karateka, so be it. But if not that Karateka is going to keep attacking that opponent with elbows, knees, roundhouse kicks, axe kicks, jumping reverse punches, jabs, and spinning back fists until that opponent is knocked out. There are no cowards in Karate. Everyone in a Karate Dojo has fought multiple times against multiple opponents in multiple weight classes. Every Karate Black Belt has been trained thoroughly in the use of distance and timing to defeat an opponent. If Karate wasn't successful on the street, it would not be successful in

SHINZEN KARATE

MMA competitions like the UFC. Karate Black Belt Lyota Machida dominated the UFC because of his excellent timing and superb range. Karate Black Belts like Lyota Machida and Georges St.Pierre dominated over there respective divisions because of their Karate base style that they used so effectively to destroy their opponents with. Spinning back kicks, jumping reverse punches, and incredibly powerful leg roundhouse kicks were used by both St. Pierre and Machida to take out their opponents with ease. It was in the Karate Dojo that both Machida and St.Pierre received their instruction in real time sparring. It was this knowledge coupled with their actual experience in sparring in Karate that provided them the base to add new skills to compete in MMA competitions like the UFC. Fighters like Georges St.Pierre have proven beyond a shadow of a doubt of the superiority of Karate in MMA competitions. This is because Karateka have a superior understanding of the use of

SHINZEN KARATE

timing and distance in a fight. It is easier to tackle a dummy than it is to kick a moving head. Karateka train to fight opponents at a distance which allows them to hit the moving opponent at a distance. People love to talk about Bruce Lee and his supposed fights against Karate fighters. There has never been a single fight of Bruce Lee that has been seen by anyone. Everyone has seen Karate fighter Andy Hug fight in K-1. It is known where Andy Hug got his Black Belt. What Black Belt did Bruce Lee have? Who gave Bruce Lee a Black Belt? He never even finished his training with Ip Man and even so, Ip Man didn't give him any certificate or award to teach. Bruce Lee pointed out the uselessness of Wing Chun after Bruce Lee was beaten badly by Kung Fu fighter Hong Man Jack in San Francisco and put in a hospital for nearly 6 months. If Wing Chun worked in a fight, it would be used in MMA. If Wing Chun worked in MMA, it would be used in street fights. Propaganda movies like Ip Man tried to show one person

SHINZEN KARATE

defeating 10 Karate Black Belts. An absurd scene in an otherwise enjoyable action movie. It was a great movie but it was just a movie. Movies are not reality. Movies are a dramatization of an individual's life. Nothing more and nothing less. Watching a movie and believing what you see is real is like watching a magic show and believing the magician is really making items disappear. Just because you saw the elephant in the room disappear does not mean that the elephant actually disappeared. Martial Arts that make public displays of trickery are to be attested and called out for what they are, a fraudulent martial art. In one demonstration by an English Wing Chun teacher which I will not name, the said teacher was asking students to attempt to break his arm. The "unbendable arm" trick was used where students are unable to break the teachers arm because they are not properly aligning the fulcrum and leverage to do so causing the students to believe that the arm is unbreakable. It is a magic trick, pure and simple. Another demonstration by the so-called Wing Chun teachers is the breaking of concrete. The concrete slab being broken is supposed to represent the human bone. How concrete could represent the human bone is a question that remains to be answered. The femur bone of the human body, for example, has a tensile strength that is 12 times stronger than concrete. IF the human femur bone is 12 times stronger than concrete, then how could breaking concrete be representative of the conditions of the human body? Breaking is just a tool for focus and concentration. If breaking is presented as a sign of the strength of a martial art, then it is being done in a disingenuous and fraudulent manner. The practice of many of these Wing Chun schools verges more on Cult like behavior than anything else. Dogmatism runs rampant, demagoguery is the rule, and teacher worship makes the students in to blind followers. There has never been an

SHINZEN KARATE

instance of a Wing Chun fighter winning a UFC championship or any MMA Championship. Never. It has never happened. There are many Karate Champions that have become Ultimate Fighting Championship Champions like Georges St.Pierre, Bas Rutten, and Chuck Lidell. The majority of fighters in all Mixed Martial Arts come from a Karate background. There are over 100 Million Karateka (practitioners of Karate) worldwide. That makes Karate the world's most popular Martial Art. Brazilian Jiu-Jitsu fighters are quick to make fun of Karate by showing videos of an ape kicking a pad. Cute but nonsensical. The Gracies were students of a Japanese man named Maeda who was an economic mission from Japan in Brazil. No one of the Gracie Family ever received a Black Belt from Maeda. Maeda was a representative of Judo and was appointed by Jigoro Kano to teach Judo. Maeda never gave anyone in Brazil a Black Belt. It is funny that people like the Gracie

SHINZEN KARATE

Family that gave themselves Black Belts laugh at Karate. Karate has proven itself in their beloved UFC multiple times. No one denies the efficiency of a rear naked choke or a Juji-Gatame (arm-bar) since many Japanese Karate teachers have been trained in Judo since they were children. Judoka Hidehiko Yoshida soundly defeated Royce Gracie in Pride Shockwave competition in 2002 in Japan by choking him out. Japanese are not awed by submission techniques introduced by Westerners because the Japanese invented the submission techniques currently being used by Westerners. Kazushi Sakuraba, a Japanese catch wrestler, defeated Royce Gracie, Royler Gracie, and Renzo Gracie by submission, because Sakuraba trained Judo since he was a child. There was nothing new that the Gracies were going to do that Sakuraba had not seen 500 plus times since he was a child practicing Judo. The hype surrounding these fights were tremendous and the shockwaves of the results were felt

SHINZEN KARATE

throughout the entire Mixed Martial Arts world. The myth of BJJ was shattered by a Catch Wrestler (Kazushi Sakuraba) and an Olympic medal winning Judoka (Hidehiko Yoshida). The BJJ guys love Muay Thai but hate Karate. Karate fighters, all of them, dominate Muay Thai fighters with ease. K1 legend Andy Hug is proof of it. Karate has proven itself against all styles with success. Have Karate fighters lost? Of course. Anyone can lose against anyone. That is just the reality of fighting. But a Karateka is a Martial Artist which means they are not a tool for cock-fighting. A Karateka is first and foremost about peace. Why do critics of Karate make fun of it while denying the many MMA Champions that have come out of Karate? It is because Karate is authentic and Japanese in nature. It is because Karate is traditional but also an Olympic sport. It is difficult to ridicule an Olympic sport but these so-called MMA experts never lose a chance to do so. The list of Karate fighters that have won MMA championships is over

SHINZEN KARATE

100 Champions. Karate will continue growing in popularity because it is an effective fighting art that has proven itself in MMA competitions, in the street, in the Dojo, and in military application. The U.S. Army has specifically practiced Karate for well over 70 years because Karate is an effective combat art, on and off the battlefield. Critics of Karate will continue their attacks because Karate is highly successful in fighting. Karate is not a meditation art. Karate evolved from the Shaolin Temple in China, who were the greatest martial artists the world has ever witnessed. The Japanese military have practiced Karate for nearly 100 years. Its effectiveness is beyond any doubt and its strikes have the ability to drop a 1 ton bull In fact, Sosai Masutatsu Oyama would knockout a 1 ton Bull to demonstrate the strength of Karate. Mas Oyama was challenged by many opponents whom he soundly defeated. Over 270 challengers faced Mas Oyama in street fight style

SHINZEN KARATE

competition with little or no rules, what would be referred to as "Vale Tudo" in modern times. Oyama nearly knocked all of them out with just one punch and no fight lasted over 3 minutes. Karate is called by some as "Japanese Boxing" and its straight forward jab and reverse punch are hard to counter. Karate was created as an art of life and death. Islanders constantly under attack had to improvise and refine their techniques so as to be applicable against invaders. If the techniques worked against trained armed soldiers, the techniques will work all the more easily against un-trained un-armed thugs. Karate training is hard and builds strength and power in the body of its practitioner. Weights are not used. The human body is the best weight you can use. Isometric exercises build up the body to have immense power in a confrontation. Karate has proven itself time after on the dojo, in the octagon, in the ring, and in the street. Georges St.Pierre proved beyond a shadow of any doubt of the efficiency of

SHINZEN KARATE

Karate inside of an octagon. Superior understanding and application of distance and timing was learned first in the Karate dojo before it was applied in the octagon. Incidentally, Ne-Waza (Ground Grappling) has been practiced in Japan for approximately 2000 years before the first UFC event in America. Karate fighters should learn to avoid takedowns and learn basic Ground Grappling to counter BJJ. The point of the Karateka is to stand and finish the opponent. It would be considered an act of cowardice to lay on your back (lay and pray) hoping that the opponent will reveal any opening to you. If you are a Karateka in a street fight and you are taken to the ground, your first move should be to stand up. The ground in the street is probably made up of hard concrete or asphalt and could cause serious bodily and head injury. Worse than this, your opponent may have friends that will attempt to attack you while you are on the ground. The ground is a place to quit, not a

SHINZEN KARATE

place to start. The Karateka should seek to avoid the ground altogether and focus on attacking the enemy in a standing position. If your opponent will not stand up, it is more than sufficient for you to verbally dress them down for being a coward that is laying on their back and waiting. If they still refuse to stand up and continue to choose to fight off their back, then you can simply stand over them and kick their legs. If they don't mind being kicked, that is good, keep kicking. Kick their legs until they are really unable to stand again. An opponent that can't stand, can't fight. Karate was tested on battlefields full of armed samurai. Do humans expect Karateka to be frightened of a few submission techniques that are applied with difficulty? Karateka don't tap out voluntarily. A Karateka stops when the fight is completed and the opponent is finished. Karateka are trained in willpower and to never quit in the face of an opponent. There are no Karateka that are cowards. Karateka are trained in the values

SHINZEN KARATE

of Courage, Compassion, Honor, and Respect. These values empower Karateka to defeat their bigger and stronger opponents without fear or hesitation. Karateka were not tall fighters so they depended on the mastering and distance and timing to defeat their larger opponents. The taller the opponent, the easier it is to enter inside their punching guard and strike them. The taller the opponent, the easier it is strike their legs without them being able to react in a quick enough time to make the attack miss. Tall fighters face a serious disadvantage against shorter fighters and that is because taller fighters are less coordinated and not as fast as shorter fighters. Either way, whether they are a tall fighter or a short fighter, without the mastery of timing and distance that is only gained from real time sparring, it will be difficult for either to effectively attack their opponent. It is important to note that MMA conflicts with the spirit of Karate. Karate, it is true became popular because of

SHINZEN KARATE

competition, but competition does not define the sport of Karate. Karateka, and their practices, define the sport of Karate. MMA calls itself a sport but it is not really a sport. It is a competition, just like a Karate competition, except that ground grappling and ground submissions have been allowed. Boxing, approximately 200 years ago, also contained grappling and submissions on the ground. But MMA is a competition and it is the competition that defines MMA. Does that make it bad? No and this is why Karate was able to excel in UFC competitions, because Karate was also built on competition. There are over 100 million Karate practitioners on earth but not all of them are MMA fans. Likewise, all MMA fans might not be Karate fans, but MMA fans love watching punching and kicking which are two features of every Karate tournament. Karate is making a resurgence this century because Karate is applicable in the street and the in the dojo. Karate has been tested in combat, tested in the

SHINZEN KARATE

octagon, and tested in MMA competitions. The growth of Karate will continue as more MMA fans become aware that the majority of MMA champions have come from a Karate background. The growth of Karate will continue as MMA fans learn more about their favorite fighters like Georges St.Pierre and UFC legends like Bas Rutten. Karate evolved from combat, was perfected in peace, and has been used by soldiers of nearly all armies since World War II. If it did not work, it would be discarded and gotten rid of, as is the fate of obsolete martial arts. Karate will evolve and has evolved, just like any other martial art in the 21st century. Karate always incorporated Kansetsu Waza (Joint Locking Techniques) from its very inception. Karate always contained throwing and sweeping techniques. Karate always contained punching techniques (Karate means empty hand) and was referred to as Japanese Boxing. Karate fighters did street fight to test their skills against unarmed opponents. The punching

SHINZEN KARATE

techniques of Karate made it an ancient
form of Boxing and the powerful Kicking
techniques of Karate like the Gedan
Mawashi Geri (leg roundhouse kick) made it
a style that was difficult to defeat and easy
to get beaten by. Karate Black Belts (real
ones not the ones in the McDojos) earned
their Black Belt through difficulty and
through trial by fire. They were bruised,
roughed up, beaten, made tired, and put
through multiple challenges before they
received any promotion, let alone a Black
Belt. A Black Belt in Karate symbolizes a
person that has mastered their character,
mastered their body, and mastered their
mind in the values and ways of Karate.
Karate used for anything other than noble
purposes make Karate in to a Bully Art that
is to be loathed. Karate is about peace and
can only be used to defend justice. If Karate
Black Belts act in an aggressive and rough
manner, than they did not allow the
teachings of Karate to transform their
characters in to one that craves harmony

and peace. Harmony and peace are the highest goals of a Karateka and it is through the constant hard training that the minds and bodies of Karateka are transformed. Changed by the hard training of Karate. Karate builds better characters because the hard training of Karate forms the body and chisels away the ego from the mind. If Karateka want to reach a higher level in their physical training, they must first reach a higher mental level through their training. The mind controls the body and the lazy body and mind can only be woken through its physical training.

CHAPTER SEVEN - MOKUSO

Mokuso is an important tool for clearing the mind in order to begin training or before sparring. Mokuso involves sitting in seated kneeling position (seiza) and deep breathing. Breathing high up in your lungs and breathing out while contracting (tightening) the abdomen muscles. Mokuso strengthens your lungs, clears your mind,

SHINZEN KARATE

and prepares you for the hard training of Karate. Traditional Japanese music could be used to play in the background to set the atmosphere. Quiet and tranquility is the goal which the ultimate goal being the quieting of the mind. This prepares the mind and the body to perform at an optimal level during the training and/or sparring that is to follow. Karate and the practice of Karate is about this. Peace, tranquility, and harmony. Achieving balance so as to be soft on the outside but hard on the inside. Mokuso should be used in every training session because it helps to calm your mind before a rigorous and complete training session. Karateka that use Mokuso have a clear advantage over those that abstain from its use. Karate should be practiced in a peaceful and quiet environment that allows for the progression and refinement of techniques under harmonious conditions. Conflict is not harmonious but it is the goal of the Karateka to make it harmonious by defeating the opponent in a graceful manner. The mind must be at peace to defeat the opponent in a graceful (peaceful) manner.

Simultaneous Attack & Defense

Karate is the art of simultaneous attack and defense. Every attack is a defense and every defense is an attack. There are many defensive blocks that are offensive in nature when performed with strength and power. Every attack is a defense that pushes back the opponent, making the opponent unable to launch any attack thereby creating a "defense" for you. The goal of Karate is simultaneous attack and defense, striking and blocking in synchronicity and sequence in order to fend off the opponent. Fending off the opponent is the only goal of a confrontation because an opponent is not to be destroyed, the Karate should only be used in self-defense to fend off the opponent so that you and your loved ones could survive. Simultaneous attack and defense allows

SHINZEN KARATE

you to string together offensive and defensive techniques in order to defeat an opponent. Each block is transformed in to attack that puts the opponent on the defensive, causing them to retreat or have to block. Karateka have to practice stringing together the many offensive and defensive maneuvers by practicing them using 8 Directional Sparring or against one opponent or many opponents, but without doing so the Karateka will not develop the workable proficiency to use simultaneous attack and defense in a real time street or dojo confrontation. No one in the history of the world has learned Karate from a book or from a YouTube video. Simultaneous attack and defense takes careful consideration and real time spent practicing putting together the techniques. Think of each technique in Karate as a letter of the Alphabet. Now think of combination techniques as putting together sentences. The various offensive and defensive techniques have to be put together with timing, distance, and form in order to have any efficiency in real time fighting.

CHAPTER EIGHT - SPARRING TIPS

Changing Rhythm – Change up the tempo and pace of your attacks in order to create confusion for your opponent.

Feinting – Use false attacks in order to setup the actual strike to be used.

Tae Sabaki – Circle your opponent in order to off-balance them.

First Strike – Take the initiative and attack in sparring. Don't wait for your opponent.

Spar Realistically – Spar your opponent in a manner that would be applicable in a real confrontation.

Create Openings – If the opponent doesn't allow you an opening to strike, create an opening by using combination strikes.

SHINZEN KARATE

Spar Safely – Always use safety headgear, mouthpiece, shinguard/footguard, etc to prevent injuries during training. Most injuries that occur are during training. Use the proper safety equipment to prevent accidents. It is also very important to train safely in a manner that does not cause bodily harm to either Karateka. Training should be muted (using less power) without it affecting the speed.

Respect Your Opponent – The point of sparring is for both Karateka to learn how to use their offensive and defensive maneuvers in real time. The point is not to hurt or destroy your opponent. The point is to learn while helping your opponent learn.

Check the Ego – Anger has no place in a Dojo. The Dojo is a place of peace. The goal of Karate is peace, internally as well as externally.

Refine yourself – The greater time you spar, the better you will be able to attack and defend. It is important to consciously refine your techniques and tactics and adapt them to the opponent you are facing.

Have Courage – It is important to be brave and courageous when facing an opponent. If you are scared, so is your opponent. Have courage and you will be successful even if you lose.

Use Techniques That Work – In any case, sparring in real time will show you the techniques that do work and the techniques that do not work.

Think Constantly – If you are not thinking constantly during sparring, then you are putting yourself at seriously bodily risk. When you stop thinking, this causes you to become complacent. Muscle memory will guide you but you must control your muscles by thinking constantly. You have to keep thinking and strategizing while you are engaged in confrontation with your opponent. Failure to keep thinking could put you in a position where you are being out-flanked or outmaneuvered by your opponent.

Post-Fight Analysis – After the sparring session, it is important to reflect upon the techniques used in blocking and attack. It is important to honestly review your performance and that of your opponent. The post-fight analysis should be done by one or more individuals so that a well-balanced review can be initiated. You should be brutally honest and completely forthright with yourself about your own performance. By doing so, you will be able to understand better the areas that are in need of improvement.

It Is Not Over – Just because you performed less than what you expected does not mean that you can't perform better next time. The key is to understand that training in Karate is a journey which takes time and the development of your skills occur over time, not overnight. If any person earned a

SHINZEN KARATE

legitimate Black Belt in Karate, they did so by making all the mistakes that a person can make. A person that has made all the mistakes can be called a Master because they understand what mistakes not to repeat. The one sparring session or 20 sparring sessions you had will teach you how to spar the 100th sparring session you have.

CHAPTER NINE - SPARRING VS REAL FIGHTING

Sparring is done either as Jiyu Ippon Kumite (Controlled Point Sparring) or as Jiyu Kumite (Free Sparring). The techniques you will have practiced you will master by practicing them in sparring. Sparring is controlled fighting. It is done as a demonstration of each Karateka's ability. Real fighting is different than sparring in that you will not be in a Dojo and you may be facing several opponents that mean to actually harm you. Losing is not an option in a real fight. Winning in a real fight means staying alive

SHINZEN KARATE

and protecting your loved ones. Winning in a Karate tournament means scoring points (ippons) in order to win a trophy or a medal. This is why Sparring is different than Real Fighting. In a real fight on the street, you could trip and fall, causing yourself serious pain. If you slip and fall while performing a spinning hook kick (ushiro mawashi geri) in the Dojo, the worst that will happen is that your pride may get hurt. If you slip and fall while performing a spinning hook kick on the street, you could seriously hurt yourself on the rough and incongruent concrete ground. In sparring, you may just be able to pull off one strike attacks or simple two strike combinations. In the street, if you are facing multiple attackers, you will be required to string together 5 or more techniques in combination (offensive and defensive) in order to survive a confrontation. Sparring is done for practice but real fighting is done for survival. While sparring in a Dojo, you expect the opponent to fight in a fair and

SHINZEN KARATE

calculated manner. While fighting in the street, you should expect the opponent to fight in a chaotic and un-fair manner. Fast paced Jiyu Kumite (Free Sparring) is as close to fighting as you will get in a Dojo. In the street, the opponent may seek to break a bottle over your head or hit you while you are on the ground. You should not expect the opponent to fight fairly and you should expect the opponent to take advantage of every opportunity to defeat you. In the Dojo, there are certain rules of respect and etiquette that are followed and there are higher ranking students watching that would prevent any type of un-fair fight. In addition the Sensei would be watching and no such street like scuffle would take place in their sight. In the street, there would be no Sensei watching over you and the only people that are going to break up the fight are the Police. The Police may just arrive when you are subduing the opponent causing the Police to think that you are the aggressor. It is unfortunate that the modern

SHINZEN KARATE

world features so many oppressors that play victim when they are called to account for carrying out oppression. Karate was developed for the development of peace and it is still a tool for ensuring self-defense, whether on the street or in the Dojo. It is a poor excuse to not stop a criminal attacking you because you might get mistakenly charged with a crime. In a confrontation on the street, if a person threatens your life or the life of your family, they are an enemy and the use of Karate would be both justified and legitimate. A Police Officer could rule however they please, but the Police Officer is not the Judge, Jury and Executioner. A Police Officer is a Peace Officer hired by the City to ensure the safety and security of the residents of that City. If you are guilty of a crime, let the Judge tell you that you are guilty of a crime. If you were justified in protecting (not killing or destroying or hurting) the lives of your family in self-defense and you only used the amount of force necessary to

SHINZEN KARATE

protect them, then you will be correct in having done so by law. If you use excess or excessive force in your own self-protection, then you could be charged with a crime and the penalties could be severe. The point is that Karateka do not have to use an excessive amount of force to subdue an opponent. Kansetsu Waza (joint locking techniques) such as a wrist lock could just as easily be used by Karate to subdue an opponent. Karateka can strike an opponent in to submission as well without having to hit them multiple times. A well placed reverse punch to the abdomen or floating rib could drop an opponent just as easily as a shoulder lock. Not all street confrontations are equal and not all confrontations require the same amount of force for self-defense. The Karateka will have to gauge the amount of force to use on the street for protection without landing themselves in legal trouble. In any case, it is the Karateka's legal obligation to retreat and to keep retreating in public view. If the

SHINZEN KARATE

opponent keeps pushing or forcing your retreat without giving you space, then you can defend yourself, but only with enough force to create the space required for your family's personal safety. Karate is not a blunt instrument created to thrash opponents to death. It is a crime to attack someone. Karate was created and developed purely as a means of self-defense. A criminal will not care or respect who your Sensei is or what Kata you have studied. In the street, the opponent will mercilessly attack you and they will seek to fight un-fairly. It is your training in Sparring that will prepare to the best of your abilities but that may not be enough if you are attacked by 4 or 5 criminals. The best thing that you can do is to train in Drills like the 8 Directional Sparring Drill and to develop your stamina to a level that will allow you to train constantly and regularly. The more you train and the harder you train, the more you will be ready for a real confrontation in the street. The point of a

SHINZEN KARATE

confrontation on the street is to survive, that is all. The winner is the person that survives the confrontation. If both parties to the conflict, then both of them won. In reality there is no winner in a confrontation, many have argued that both parties to a confrontation are losers and this may be the more accurate statement of the two. The only point is to survive and ensure the safety and survival of your loved ones. If that means subduing the opponent, then so be it. If that means running away, then so be it. You do not lose face by retreating. You save lives by retreating. You save lives by pursuing peace rather than conflict through confrontation. In any case, it is your duty to retreat in the face of conflict so that you will have given the aggressor the signal that you do not want to fight. If the aggressor attacks you or your family, then you have every right to defend yourself using the same amount of force which the aggressor used against you. This is fair and understandable because it prevents the

SHINZEN KARATE

creation of lawlessness through vigilantism and other illegal means. Karate provides the perfect means to deal with an aggressor on the street. If you are attacked by a drunken aggressor (as is the case regularly on a typical Friday night in America or the UK), then you have the right to block the punch and sweep their leg. You do not have the right to use an excessive amount of force that would bring legal penalties for your person. You could punch them if they punch you back but then you both could arrested for fighting in public. Karate allows the Karateka to use just the right amount of force needed without resorting to violent techniques that would be deemed excessive. That is one of the hallmarks of Karate, the ability to meet every situation with an answer. The answer to violence would never be more violence. If you are attacked, you can defend, you can subdue the opponent using Kansetsu Waza (joint locking techniques), but it would be illegal for you to hurt the aggressor in an excessive manner. Karate is about harmony and peace, something the aggressor doesn't understand. Karateka are interested in peace and harmony through the practice of traditional martial arts. It would not be morally correct for a Karate Black Belt to use their training and skills for anything other than peace, inside and outside of the Dojo.

Kaizen

Kaizen is the Japanese concept of incremental improvement. Making major leaps in progress is difficult to achieve without passing every little step along the way. Small improvements that are introduced on a daily basis make you progress. The Japanese concept of Kaizen drives the Karateka to make small step by step improvements in their sparring, in their training practices, and in their forms. Through Kaizen, the Karateka will see the larger improvements they are hoping for by following the smaller steps to reach that

SHINZEN KARATE

goal. It is similar to breaking down one's goals in to smaller goals except that you are breaking down your overall progress in to smaller progressions. Each daily progression allows you to move one step closer in your overall progression as a Karateka. Kaizen boosts your growth and allows you to achieve a methodical and organized form of progress because it is done in a calculated manner. Use Kaizen and its wisdom of daily evolution and progress in your skills as a Karateka. Understanding Karate entails first understanding the Japanese culture and the Japanese mind that developed the ancient martial art of Karate. If Karateka like Sosai Masutatsu Oyama achieved greatness and legendary status in the practice of Karate, it is because they used the Japanese principles that defined Karate to excel in their martial arts abilities. Kaizen is a major part of your training toolbox for advancing.

SHINZEN KARATE

CHAPTER TEN – KARATE PHILOSOPHY

Karate is an art of peace and harmony with the environment. Karateka pride themselves on the development of the personal character and the promotion of the values that make up Karate. These values are:

Courage, Compassion, Honor, and Respect

Courage is the most important piece of this formula, for without courage it would not be possible for you to achieve anything at all. It is important to understand that nothing happens on its own. It is because of your insistence that something materializes. Courage pushes you to reach for more and to achieve more. Courage makes you motivated and able to press forward in the face of all types of difficulties. You have to have courage if you want to be a Karateka. It takes courage to train. It takes courage to spar an opponent. It takes courage to compete in a tournament. It takes courage

SHINZEN KARATE

to stop a criminal from hurting you or your family. It takes courage to stop a crime when you are witnessing it. Courage is the first principle of Shinzen Karate philosophy.

Compassion is required of a Karateka, for without compassion, Karate would turn in to a bully art. Compassion makes the Karateka able to understand his opponent. Compassion makes the Karateka able to feel what the opponent is feeling. Compassion causes the Karateka to have mercy on the opponent. Compassion causes the Karateka to feel the nuances in an opponent's movement. Compassion makes the Karateka a fighter for good rather than a bully for bad. Compassion makes the Karateka an individual to be looked up to. Compassion makes the Karateka understand themselves better so that they will be able to better their opponents better. A Karateka that lacks compassion will become cruel and mean. Karateka have to melt in to society and be a natural defender of justice and good. If Karateka become mean and cruel, they will become useless to society. Karateka have to be a force of good for society and the way to do that is by having compassion for others. A person that is lacking in compassion for others will do mean things that hurt others. A Karateka with compassion becomes an individual that is respected and loved. Honor plays a huge part in the philosophical pantheon of a Karateka. Honor makes the Karateka forthright and upright. Honor makes the Karateka act in a manner that would not bring shame to Karate or to themselves. Karateka believe Honor to be a major part of their lives and that a dishonorable Karateka is not worthy of wearing a Black Belt. When a Karateka wears a Black Belt, they are representing their Sensei and their school (ryu). If they act in a manner that is contrary to the teachings of their Sensei, that would be considered dishonorable and it would be considered an act that would bring shame

SHINZEN KARATE

to them. Understanding Karate is as much about understanding the Asian mind and how it operates. Honor plays a huge role in Karate and it is important to respect your opponent and to respect their Sensei. It is important to always act in a manner that would bring good and positive light your Sensei. The most important thing in Karate is honoring your Sensei and honoring their Masters before them. Bowing plays a huge part in a Dojo because when a Karateka bows, they are honoring the Sensei and the senior students. The Karateka honor each other and honor their Sensei collectively. Honor drives the action of a Karateka inside and outside of the Dojo and it is so important for a beginning Karateka to take the principle of honor seriously. A Karateka lacking honor could never be judged as a serious teacher regardless of their skill level. Karate was built on honor and will continue developing in honor as long as traditional Karate is practiced. Karateka respect other Karateka. Karateka also

SHINZEN KARATE

respect other styles as well but that does not mean that Karateka will tolerate misinformation or lies when it comes to the history of various martial arts. Karateka respect the traditions and culture of Japan which is why Japanese traditions are so heavily ingrained in a Karate dojo, no matter where the Dojo is located. Karateka respect the Dojo, the Sensei, the senior students and lower ranked students of the Dojo. Karate thrives on respect and its practice is entwined in to the practices of the Dojo. Karateka respect the Belt that each Karateka earned along the way and they respect the process by which they learn the ancient art of Karate. Respect keeps the Karateka able to act in a correct manner and respect builds the moral fortitude of the Karateka. Karateka that fail to practice respect are no different than bullies or thugs that randomly attack people. The difference between a Karateka and a bully is that a Karateka has respect for life while the bully has a disdain for humans

SHINZEN KARATE

(which is itself a disdain for life). Karateka respect each other by bowing when they enter a Dojo, bowing when they face each other for sparring, bow after they finish sparring, and bow when they leave the dojo. Karate begins and ends with respect. The Karate Philosophy is about Courage, Compassion, Honor, and Respect. These 4 Principles guide a Karateka to develop their character and to become a better person through training. All 4 principles are important and should be applied to create a complete Karateka. Karateka should take all 4 seriously and implement them inside and outside of the Dojo so as to achieve balance.

CHAPTER ELEVEN - DEALING WITH BULLIES

It could happen at any time. I was chased by a gang on Burbank Blvd in the Woodland Hills area of the San Fernando Valley of Los Angeles. You could be chased and attacked for what you are wearing, who you are walking with, or for whatever the criminal or criminals choose that day. This is one of the unfortunate realities of life. I have been randomly attacked walking out of a party for no other reason than the criminal didn't like the way I looked. I have had a criminal in Santa Monica threaten to beat me up and rape my family over laundry. I have been randomly attacked in a fast food parking lot by criminals thugs for no other reason than they didn't like where I was eating. I have been attacked by false Martial Arts teachers for no other reason than they wanted to ego trip and prove their fighting prowess. I have been confronted by muggers right in front of the Eiffel Tower in Paris, France. There are many more stories but you get the picture. Humans are not always nice and are not always polite. In fact, humans are self-serving individuals that only think of their own interest. The world is chaotic because human nature is chaotic causing humans to act in a chaotic manner. If all persons followed the laws as they are written out then there would be no need

SHINZEN KARATE

for Police. Unfortunately, by the time the Police arrive it may be too late. You have to be able to defend yourself in the face of an aggressor. It doesn't matter if you don't win, all that matter s is that they don't win. If they don't win and can't beat you, it is as good as a loss for them. As I have witnessed firsthand, when they can't beat you, they may end up crying and apologizing, as happened to me. Standing up to a bully will make that bully think twice about confronting you again. If the aggressor knows they will receive a bloody nose if they attack you, then they will not attack you or threaten you anymore. Humans wants to show their strength and power over others which is why they bully other humans. It is a vicious cycle because there is always another bully stronger waiting to bully that bully. Regardless of how strong the opponent is, it would not be correct for you to allow them to bully you. People like to bully others but when someone stands up to their bullying, the

SHINZEN KARATE

bully reveals themselves to be the coward that we always knew they were. Bullies never make it far in life, but nice people do. Karateka follow a code of courage, compassion, honor, and respect while bullies only think of oppression. The best method for pushing back a bully is with a warning that you will defend yourself if pushed again. Bullies get away with whatever they can get away with and that is what makes them bullies. They are lawless at heart and do not respect authority or the law. Karate is your weapon to deal with a bully. If they want a fight, give them a fight. Next time, they will not be so eager to prove how strong they are while using you as an example to scare others. Bullies are cowards that break down and cry or become silent after you have to stood up to them. They are loud and barking like a dog in your face but once you stand up to them they become like lambs. Until bullies realize that their behavior is not acceptable, they will continue bullying others. Karate is a

SHINZEN KARATE

tool that empowers you to stand up to the bully and to stand up to their oppression. The Founder of Shotokan Karate Gichin Funakoshi said "Karate should only be used for justice". That statement is representative for all Karate and should be the guiding line in the behavior of all Karateka. Bullies use their fists (and other body parts) to oppress humans. Some bullies use a pen to oppress humans. Regardless of the tool they use, a bully is detestable in nature because their very modus operandi depends on the use of bullying to berate and devalue others. Karate gives you the self-confidence to stand up to a bully. If they are going to verbally berate you, then you should inform that you will not tolerate being talked too in that manner. If they raise their hands on you, then you have every right to defend yourself to the extent that it will ensure the survival of yourself and your family. Karate is a tool for self-defense with the ability to transform the person being bullied in to an

SHINZEN KARATE

individual that is capable of defending. themselves. Bullies are not attracted to Karate because bullies live by a code of criminality while Karateka lived by the code of Courage, Compassion, Honor, and Respect. Karate was built on the code of Bushido and the values of Japanese culture define Karate. The values of lawlessness, criminality, and chaos define the bully. The bully could be 7 feet tall and the Karateka could be 5 feet tall and the Karateka would still stand up to the bully. In fact, it is much easier to use Karate if you are 5 feet tall, giving that 5 feet tall Karateka a distinct fighting advantage over the 7 footer. It is not about height, weight, race, class, or anything else. It is about that Karateka are trained to fight constantly and a bully is an easy opponent to be taken apart in a confrontation. Bullies feel like they have achieved something by putting others in a position of terror. In fact, bullies did achieve something and that is the achievement of being hated by most humans. Karateka

SHINZEN KARATE

stand up to bigger and stronger opponents all the time therefore a Karateka would have no problem beating a bully inside and outside the Dojo. The Karateka is trained to do and is prepared to do so at anytime. A Karate Black Belt experienced many bruises before achieving their Black Belt. A Karate Black Belt has to fight often and most certainly has to fight another Karate Black Belt in the Black Belt test. A Black Belt became a Karate Black Belt because they are able to fight and because they have a standard level of proficiency in the Karate syllabus laid out by their Sensei. A Karate Black Belt that is not able to fight is not representative of Karate. Karate is a fighting art that was created in a tense volatile situation, that of being invaded by foreigners. Karate empowered the Okinawans to defend themselves in the face of stronger and better equipped invaders from both Japan and China. Their Karate had to be perfect or else it would fail them when they needed to survive using it. The

SHINZEN KARATE

Karate of the Okinawans was good enough to protect the unarmed people of Okinawa from foreign occupation as well as to protect their farms and villages. Karate would deal with a bully like any other bully, a Karateka would offer the bully the chance to give up on their conquest. If the bully persisted, the Karateka would use the necessary force to restrain the criminal bully until the criminal bully retreated or was handed over to the law for further prosecution. Karateka frequently served as Police because their knowledge of martial arts and their character training in courage, compassion, honor, and respect made them effective peacekeepers among locals. Karateka in Okinawa that trained even infrequently were able to beat and defeat their more equipped counterparts. Karate was built on fighting just like modern Mixed Martial Arts was built on fighting with the difference being that Karate is a martial art with emphasis on things like character development. Karateka served as local

SHINZEN KARATE

authorities because their Karate training made them able to easily deal with multiple opponents without fright and with certainty. Just like how the Kung Fu practitioners of the Shaolin Temple in China at one time served as soldiers for China, Karateka in Japan at one time served as soldiers for Japan. Modern day bullies are no different than ancient day bullies. All the bullies have a false sense of pride and a weak constitution. Karateka have a strong will, a strong constitution, and are not afraid of any opponent inside or outside the Dojo. Kyokushin Karateka or Shinzen Karateka will fight any opponent if that is what the opponent wants. Karateka earn their Belts in testing by fighting in front of the Sensei. A Karateka that cannot fight cannot be called a true Karateka. All Karateka have to fight frequently in the Dojo to get their Belt because in the official testing for their Belts, there will be Ippon Jiyu Kumite (Point Sparring) or Jiyu Kumite (Free Sparring). Some Belts have to fight up

SHINZEN KARATE

to 3 opponents in their testing. Karate has Kata as its base but fighting is what makes Karateka experienced to be able to have real fighting experience. Both Kata and Sparring are equally important and each one compliments the other. Kata is a form of walking meditation that puts the Karateka in a zen like state that allows for the free flow of techniques and subconscious movement. Kata is the base of Karate but it is the Sparring that makes the Karateka a skilled practitioner of the fighting arts. Many MMA fighters who mistook Karate for a traditional dance experienced a rude awakening when hit with an Ushiro Mawashi Geri (Spinning Hook Kick) or with a Tobi Gyaku Tsuki (Jumping Reverse Punch). Karate didn't become the world's most popular combat sport with over 100 million Karate practitioners by being passive and weak in the fighting arts. Karate was built on fighting just as much as it was built on Kata but its emphasis has always been on

SHINZEN KARATE

character development and the betterment of the human character. The modern times has revealed many ugly human characters that have sought to hurt other humans with violence. Karate empowers you as the human to protect yourself and your family if you are in an unarmed life and death type situation. It is not the ultimate weapon in comparison to firearms, but Karate is the ultimate weapon if you are unarmed and need to protect yourself and the lives of your loved ones. Karate will give you the self confidence to stand up to the bully that is acting as an aggressor towards you. Bullies do not like humans and they cannot be taught to like other humans. They are what they are and that is small children that never grew up. A person with power will have no reason to show their power. You may be the victim of a person oppressing you or bullying you. The criminal bully might be too afraid to face you so they have to resort to bullying you from afar. They feel this gives them power over you. Bullies

SHINZEN KARATE

have no power at all which is why they feel they can gain by bullying you. They feel it makes them powerful and responsible. Bullies have to lie to gain some sense of false pride about having power and that is because they are completely powerless to begin with. If they had any power at all, they would be seeking harmony for all rather than seeking out self serving purposes like bullying. Karate empowers the Karateka to easily and quickly deal with any bully, no matter how many steroids they have used, how much creatine they have eaten, or how much performance enhance substances they have used. Karate was made for small people that are not necessarily ripped like a bodybuilder. A Karateka just needs to land one punch or one kick on the bully to remind the bully of the mistake they have made in bullying others. Bullying is a bad and ugly trait of villains. Karateka despise villains because villains use their power to hurt others.

SHINZEN KARATE

CHAPTER TWELVE – KARATE FOR CHILDREN

Karate for children should be informative, fun, and action filled. Starting from the age of 5, children can be taught Karate. The Karate should be Kata based and non-contact for safety purposes. Learning Karate at a young age could provide a great base for the student to develop their skills from. Karate for children should be understandable, easy to learn, and the techniques should be easy to execute. Karate for children should be broken down in to steps so it is easy to digest. If the moves are too complex or involve too many steps, the children will not be able to do them. The best route is to choose two or three techniques to teach each class session. You are probably wondering what this has to do with you. Whether you are a Sensei or if you are a student, at one point or another you will be required to teach lower ranked students (students that have a

SHINZEN KARATE

lower belt than you do) and they may include children. The less techniques you show them and have them practice per class session, the more successful you will be in being able to permanently instill the techniques you are teaching. Children start of with a Tabula Rasa (Blank Slate) and are able to learn everything that you teach. Their physiological abilities will catch up to their theoretical knowledge. This is why Kata is such an important tool for teaching non-contact Karate. Children can safely practice a simple Kata that they learn in the Dojo and they can practice that one Kata for months until they have mastered simple punching and simple body movement. Children above the age of 7 could engage in Ippon Jiyu Kumite (Point Sparring) with complete safety and sparring equipment including mouthpiece, headguard, gloves, and feet guards. Ippon Jiyu Kumite for children should be no more than one time per week and it should be coached and watched to prevent injuries or accidents.

SHINZEN KARATE

Karate for children should be light and fun, interesting and exciting, and fast paced and enjoyable. If Karate becomes tedious or too serious for children, then it loses their long term interest. A child arriving at a Dojo should feel that the higher ranked students as well as the Sensei are providing a safe and comfortable environment for the student to develop in. Older ranked students are viewed as people to emulate, style wise. This is why the Sensei should operate their Dojo in a manner that is conducive to positive reinforcement and positive support from the highest ranked students to the lowest ranked students. Children learning Karate should be given positive reinforcement so that they are happy about being in the Dojo. Discipline and quiet training should be the rule of the Dojo but this does not mean the Dojo should be a place that is lacking compassion. Courage, Compassion, Honor, and Respect should be the rules of the Dojo and the guiding principles of each Karateka

SHINZEN KARATE

in that Dojo. Karate runs on these principles and the higher ranked students as well as the Sensei should seek to instill these (or similar uplifting principles) in children so that they are given the self confidence to succeed. Karate instills self-confidence through the practice of these principles and the practice of martial arts. Karate can help children become happier, have greater self-esteem, as well as to make them perform better in educational tests. The reason that children perform better in school after attending Karate is that Karate builds their focus and concentration, allowing them to perform better in school. Karate for children should be taught in a way that instills values in their minds while training their bodies for self-defense. Children should start off with simple Kata and simple one-two punching maneuvers. Over time they can be worked up to Point Sparring once they have reached the age of 7. Point Sparring is touch sparring which means there is no real contact with any force that

SHINZEN KARATE

would cause injury. In contrast to Full Contact Sparring (Jiyu Kumite), Point Sparring has the Karateka land a technique without power on the other opponent. Both opponents are completely guarded with head guard, mouthpiece, gloves, shin guards, and feet guard. The Sensei and other higher ranked students watch the Ippon Jiyu Kumite (Point Sparring) and control the bout to prevent any injuries. The amount of power that is used by each Karateka in Ippon Jiyu Kumite should be minimal and the focus should be on speed and control. Any illegal strike should be met with a warning and if continued a disqualification. Safety and the security of all students should be the first priority of senior ranking students and that of the Sensei. Children practicing Karate should be given active encouragement to fill them with enthusiasm about sports and athletics. Since Karate is an Olympic sport, Karate can be a doorway for many children to grow in to adult professional athletes. The

SHINZEN KARATE

resurgence of Karate and its place as an Olympic sport will surely open many doors for Karateka in the future in industries such as Stunt Choreography, Fight Choreography, Exercise Studio Owner, Fight Promoter, Security Company Owner, or just a Personal Trainer. Karate teaches children more than punches and kicks, Karate teaches children strategies that they can use inside and outside of the Dojo. Karate teaches children to have fast reflexes and fast minds. Karate teaches children to sense danger and to fight back in the face of it. Karate gives children the needed self-confidence to perform better on educational tests. Children are better off after learning Karate and it shows in their behavior and in their scholastic achievements. Karate should be taught to children enthusiastically and children should be patiently encouraged by their parents to learn the ancient art of Karate as soon as they reach the age of 5.

SHINZEN KARATE

CHAPTER THIRTEEN – WAY OF KARATE

The way of Karate is the way of the Samurai and the way of Bushido. The way of Karate is in peace. The way of Karate is in discipline, honor, courage, compassion, respect, and charity towards others. The way of Karate is in humanitarianism. The way of Karate is in equilibrium and mental balance. The way of Karate is being one with your environment and with nature. The way of Karate is in mindfulness of your surroundings and harmony with your environment. Many martial artists are confused about whether Karate is an amalgamation of techniques or if it is an actual Way. Karate was at one time viewed as Karate Jitsu but is now viewed as Karate Do. It is a Way of life and a way of being. Karate is a way of acting and that is acting as if you are at peace with yourself and with the world. Only by being at peace with yourself and the world, will the angers and frustration leave you. The Zen teachings of

SHINZEN KARATE

just being defines how Karateka behave. Karate is a way of life and a way of self-defense. Karate is a way of harmony that brings the Karateka in to harmony with the environment. This is why much of Karate training is done in nature. The harmonization of the human with their environment allows them to better understand nature and thus better understand themselves. They become like the nature they are harmonizing with, flexible and dynamic. The Karateka should strive for these two qualities and that is to be flexible and dynamic. Flexibility makes the Karateka supple in the face of rigid conditions, yielding in the face of difficulties, and able to progress despite opposition. To be flexible in the face of opposition is what Karateka learn when they spar in the Dojo. Jiyu Kumite teaches the Karateka when to defend, when to attack, when to evade, when to yield, and when to advance. This is what makes Karateka unique. Their ability to understand

SHINZEN KARATE

the nuances in their environment and to
traverse the path they create by their own
doing. Good deeds bring good and bad
deeds bring bad. Understandable by all and
non-exclusive to any. Karateka learn the
way of Karate in order to have the
attributes or qualities that could allow them
to be both strong as well as yielding. The
best advice ever given by a Sensei was to
"run" rather than fight. Karate Ni Sente
Nashi means there is no first attack in
Karate and this is the standard that guides
Karateka in their actions. The way of Karate
is Self-Defense because there is no first
attack in Karate. A Karateka cannot and
should not ever be the initiator in a fight. A
Karateka will prevent a fight from ever
happening because that is the first part of
the Way of Karate. Way of Karate resides in
being courageous and brave, respectful and
honorable, and pliant and understanding.
There are critics of Karate that want to
capitalize on the recent MMA popularity to
speak negatively about Karate. Karate has

SHINZEN KARATE

existed for thousands of years because it came from the Shaolin Temple in China. MMA has existed as a sport for 20 years. Lets compare 20 years with 2000 years and arrive at a logical solution. Karate has a way and the Way of Karate is about harmony and peace. The Way of Karate is in effectiveness and the Way of Karate is in victory. If the Way of Karate was not in victory, then you would not have over 100 MMA Champions from a Karate background. The Way of Karate is about achieving mental and physical balance. The Way of Karate is in the creation and promotion of Peace. The Way of Karate is in being technical and functional. The Way of Karate is about defeating oneself inside the Dojo. The Way of Karate is in honoring the Karate Masters that came before you. The Way of Karate is in respect for your opponent, before and after you have engaged them. The Way of Karate is in progression through the rigorous practice of physical and mental exercise.

SHINZEN KARATE

CHAPTER FOURTEEN – COURAGE

This principle, above all principles, empowers the Karateka to stand up to an enemy that is stronger and bigger. Courage is the quality that gives the Karateka strength internally and externally. Courage is not an easy thing for a beginner to achieve. To paraphrase Sosai Masutatsu Oyama "Your opponent is not a deity. If you are scared, so is your opponent." The meaning of this is profound. Courage comes from within one's heart and cowardice also comes from within one's heart. If the opponent is stronger or bigger than you, than all the more reason for you to show how effective Karate really is. Karate was developed by short to mid height humans, making it very effective against taller opponents. Whether the opponent is large or small, courage drives you to defeat them and engage them. If the opponent attacks, then deflect and strike. If the opponent defends, then create a false opening for the opponent to strike and counter. Fighting is not a matter of mystery techniques and chanting mantras. Fighting is a matter of experience spent training fighting (Jiyu Kumite) in real time. Real time fighting builds up the courage of the fighter to be able to perform effectively in a real fight. Karateka are courageous because they have trained in preparation to have the self-confidence to face an opponent. The courage of a Karateka comes from their readiness and preparedness beforehand. If Karateka are courageous in the ring it is because they have successfully and un-successfully performed in the Dojo countless times. They have had to face taller fighters, smaller fighters, stronger fighters, and weaker fighters. The more opponents they faced, the greater courage they were able to develop because they have developed themselves in the Dojo to the extent that they could successfully defend themselves. All Karateka have trained extensively in Jiyu Kumite and have

SHINZEN KARATE

had to fight multiple opponents for their Black Belts. The Karateka developed their courage and experience in the Dojo and developed their expertise through fighting. Cowardice is non-existent in a Dojo. Any person that faces off and fights against another person deserves a minimum level of respect at the least. It takes courage to fight. It takes courage to punch, kick, duck, maneuver, and to defeat your opponent. Fighting is an art but Courage is a principle that Karateka hold highly. A courageous Karateka with less technically developed skills can still develop in to a capable martial artist. But a Karateka with highly developed punching, kicking, and blocking skills that is lacking in Courage will not be a good Karateka. Inner strength can be more important than muscular strength. Courage is more important than having big muscles. Courage is more important than having a six-pack abdomen or well-toned muscles. Courage is strictly having the strength to confront your opponent and to progress in

SHINZEN KARATE

the face of all the difficulties you are experiencing.

CHAPTER FIFTEEN – KNOW YOUR RANGE

Karateka are masters of range and they completely understand how to use range and timing to defeat their stronger and bigger opponents. There are three ranges in Karate and they are close range, mid range, and long range. It is important to understand range because you cannot use long range techniques from close range and you cannot use close range techniques from long range. To first have a basic understanding of range, you should stand in Zenkutsu Dachi with your left leg forward and hold your left arm out completely until it touches your opponent. This is the range of your jab. Now do the same with your right hand. This is the range of your reverse punch. Now do the same with your right leg, pushing it out in a roundhouse kick form until it touches your opponent. This is the range of your back leg roundhouse kick.

SHINZEN KARATE

Until you understand range and its applications, you will be able unable to use it to your advantage in a fight. Range is a matter of distance to your target and1 if your technique is not able to be used in that range because it will not hit the target, then you use another technique that fits the range of the target you're attempting to strike. The more your spend in the Dojo doing things like Jiyu Kumite and three point sparring, the more you will be able to develop an accurate sense of range. Range is the most important element of your fighting because a technique that is not able to meet its range becomes a useless technique. Karate thrives on using techniques that display grace as well as efficiency. Energy should not be wasted and the opponent's defenses should be read and probed for weaknesses. Karateka move and attack in a graceful manner. Karateka also defend against attacks in a graceful manner. Karateka do not need to waste energy on extra movements and that is because they understand range. They understand the range from which they attacking the opponent and Karateka understand the range from which they are defending against an opponent's attacks. Understanding range allows Karateka to control the pace, rhythm, and tempo of the fight and allows them to deny their opponent the opportunity to strike them. Range allows you to control the outcome of the fight, to a large extent, because you only allow your opponent as much as range as you wish. If you want, you can keep the conflict long range as well as mid range. You can also choose to just keep the conflict short range. You can freely range to confuse your opponent and to not allow them a stationary target to attack. Your range determines your success which is why you should spend considerable time attempting to master Range. By thoroughly understanding range, you will have a clear advantage over your opponent. Range is the determining factor between a

SHINZEN KARATE

technique that fails and a technique that succeeds. Study the nuances of range with concentration so that you will be able to use the techniques you've practiced efficiently and effectively.

SHINZEN KARATE

GLOSSARY

A

Atemi – Punching techniques that focus on striking vital parts.

Arigato – Thank you.

Arigato Gozaimasu – Thank you very much.

Ashi – Legs.

B

Black Belt – Signifies a martial artist's expertise in a particular style; karate, judo, jujitsu, etc.

Bokken – Wooden sword.

Bunkai – The applications of the kata.

Bushi – Warrior.

SHINZEN KARATE

Bushido – Way of the Warrior.

C

Chodan – Mid-level. Stomach area.

D

Dachi – Stance.

Dan – Ranking.

Do – Way.

Dojo – Training Hall. Literally "place of the way."

E

Empi – Elbow.

F

SHINZEN KARATE

Fudoshin – Calm Mind

G

Gedan Barai – Down block.

Geri – Kick.

Gi – Uniform.

Gichin Funakoshi – Founder of Shotokan Karate.

Go – Hard.

Goshin – Self defense.

Gyaku Tsuki – Reverse punch.

H

Hai – Yes.

Hajime – Start.

SHINZEN KARATE

Himitsu – Hidden techniques in the katas or forms.

Honbu – Headquarters. Main school.

I

Ippon – Point scored in martial arts competition. (Jp)

J

Jiyu Kumite – Free Sparring.

Jodan – Upper. Head & shoulders area.

K

Kamae – Fighting stance.

Kansetsu Waza – Joint Locking Techniques

Karate – Empty hand.

SHINZEN KARATE

Kata – Form or set of pre-defined movements that train the practitioners muscle memory.

Ki – Internal energy. Also spirit.

Kiba Datchi – Horse stance.

Kihon - Basics

Kime – Focus.

Kohai – Junior leader in a martial arts school or organization.

Kumiuchi – Ancient grappling art form.

Kyokushin – Karate style that emphasizes low powerful kicks. Founded by Mas Oyama.

Kyudo – Japanese martial art that utilizes the bow and arrow with a focus on character development.

SHINZEN KARATE

M

Mae – Front.

Makiwara – Wooden striking post used in Karate.

Matte – Stop.

Mawate – Turn Around.

Mikazuki Geri – Crescent Kick.

Mokuso – Meditation.

N

Nage – Throwing.

Ninja –Japanese mercenary assassins that were expertly trained in stealth techniques including the murdering of their opponents in their sleep.

SHINZEN KARATE

Ninjitsu – Japanese martial art that emphasizes silent attacks, invisibility, and evasions.

O

Oi – Lunge.

Osu – Greetings and respect.

R

Randori – Free Sparring.

Rei – Bow.

Ryu – Academy School.

S

Sabaki – Movement.

SHINZEN KARATE

Samurai – Feudal class of warriors during 15th century Japan. Trained in armed and unarmed combat.

Seiza – Kneeling position.

Sempai – Senior leader in a martial arts school or organization.

Sensei – Instructor. Literally means teacher.

Seppuku – Ritual of self-disembowelment carried out by samurai.

Shuto – Hand tensed in a rigid form similar to a knife. Also called knife hand.

Soto Uke – Outer hook block.

T

Tai Sabaki – Circling and body shifting.

Tatami – Training Mat.

SHINZEN KARATE

Tobi – Jumping.

U

Uchi – Inner.

Uchi Deshi – Live-in student

Uke – Block. The literal meaning is "to receive".

Ushiro – Reverse.

W

Waza – Technique.

Z

Zanshin – State of awareness.

Zenkutsu Datchi – Front status.

SHINZEN KARATE

SHINZEN KARATE

KARATE ORGANIZATIONS

North American Sport Karate Association
600 Sherwood Road
Shoreview, MN 55126
Tel: 612-799-7914
Fax: 651-490-1133
Email: NASKA_LC@msn.com

European Karate Federation
OLYMPIC CENTRE OF ANO LIOSIA
133 43 ANO LIOSIA (ATHENS)
GREECE
Tel: +30-210-6813112
Email: ekf-secretariat@wkf.net

International Sport Karate Association
14260 W. Newberry Road #341
Newberry, FL USA 32669-2765
Tel: 352-339-4376

U.S.A. Karate
1631 Mesa Avenue, Suite A
Colorado Springs, CO 80906
Tel: (719) 477-6925
Email: natoffice@usankf.org

SHINZEN KARATE

NOTES

SHINZEN KARATE

NOTES

SHINZEN KARATE

NOTES

SHINZEN KARATE

NOTES

SHINZEN KARATE

MIKAZUKI PUBLISHING HOUSE CATALOG

1) 25 Principles of Martial Arts
2) 25 Principles of Strategy
3) Arctic Black Gold
4) American Antifa
5) Art of Western Boxing
6) Back to Gold
7) Basketball Play Design Book
8) Beginner's Magician Handbook
9) Boxing Coloring Book
10) California's Next Century 2.0
11) Camping Survival Handbook
12) Captain Bligh's Voyage
13) Coming To America Handbook
14) Customer Sales Organizer
15) DIY Comic Book
16) DIY Comic Book Part II
17) Economic Collapse Survival Manual
18) Find the Ideal Husband
19) Football Play Design Book
20) Freakshow Los Angeles
21) Game Creation Manual
22) George Washington's Farewell Address

SHINZEN KARATE

23) Hagakure; Book of Tea Leaves
24) I Dream in Haiku
25) Internet Connected World
26) Irish Republican Army Manual of Guerrilla Warfare
27) Japan Coloring Book
28) John Locke's 2nd Treatise on Civil Government
29) Karate 360
30) Learning Magic
31) Living the Pirate Code
32) Los Angeles Coloring Book
33) Magic as Science and Religion
34) Magicians Coloring Book
35) Make Racists Afraid Again
36) Master Password Organizer Handbook
37) Mikazuki Jujitsu Manual
38) Mikazuki Political Science Manual
39) MMA Coloring Book
40) Mythology Coloring Book
41) Mythology Dictionary
42) Native Americana
43) Ninja Style

SHINZEN KARATE

44) Ouija Board Enigma
45) Political Advertising Manual
46) Quotes Gone Wild
47) Rapper's Rhyme Book
48) Self-Examination Diary
49) Shinzen Karate
50) Shogun X the Last Immortal
51) Stories of a Street Performer
52) Storyboard Book
53) Swords & Sails; Legacy of the Red Lion
54) Tao Te Ching
55) The Adventures of Sherlock Holmes
56) The Arrival of Palloncino
57) The Art of War
58) The Book of Five Rings
59) The Bribe Vibe
60) The Card Party
61) The History of Acid Tripping
62) The History of Aliens
63) The Man That Made The English Language
64) Tokiwa; A Japanese Love Story
65) T-Shirt Design Book

SHINZEN KARATE

66) United Nations Charter
67) U.S. Army Anti-Guerrilla Warfare Manual
68) U.S. Military Boxing Manual
69) Van Carlton Detective Agency; Burgundy Diamond
70) William Shakespeare's Sonnet's
71) Words of King Darius
72) World War Water

SHINZEN KARATE

STOP DEFORESTATION!

160 Acres of land are destroyed on earth every minute by the effects of Deforestation.

You Can Do The Following:

Plant Trees

Donate money to a Tree conservation fund

Organize a Trash (Litter) Pick-Up in your nearby nature area

Start a Recycling Drive in your neighborhood

Buy Trees and Donate Them to a Friend or Neighbor

WE ONLY HAVE ONE EARTH

www.ingramcontent.com/pod-product-compliance
Lightning Source LLC
Chambersburg PA
CBHW071532040426
42452CB00008B/985